Jonathan Goodman, the crime historian, was for some years a theatre director and television producer. As well as being the author of a number of books on criminology, he was general editor of the Celebrated Trials series and has also published four novels and a volume of poetry. He is a member of the British Academy of Forensic Sciences, the Medico-Legal Society and Our Society.

THE CHRISTMAS MURDERS

Edited by Jonathan Goodman

SPHERE BOOKS LIMITED

For Thomas M. McDade, President of
The Society of Connoisseurs in Murder

SPHERE BOOKS LTD

Published by the Penguin Group
27 Wrights Lane, London W8 5TZ, England
Viking Penguin Inc., 40 West 23rd Street, New York, New York 10010, USA
Penguin Books Australia Ltd, Ringwood, Victoria, Australia
Penguin Books Canada Ltd, 2801 John Street, Markham, Ontario, Canada L3R 1B4
Penguin Books (NZ) Ltd, 182–190 Wairau Road, Auckland 10, New Zealand

Penguin Books Ltd, Registered Offices: Harmondsworth, Middlesex, England

First published in Great Britain in 1986 by Allison & Busby Ltd
Published by Sphere Books Ltd, 1988

This collection copyright © Jonathan Goodman 1986

Printed and bound in Great Britain by
Richard Clay Ltd, Bungay, Suffolk

Contents

Murders of Christmases Past

IF CRIME STATISTICS were not as untrustworthy as are many of the people whose transgressions are branded, tallied and dissected by crime statisticians, it would be of interest, admittedly only slight, to compare a fragment of the figures headed *Murder* with my impression, recently gained, that though on Christmas Days murder will be fresh in the memory of some executants and in the final stages of premeditation by some of those who are as yet merely ambitious, the *act* of murder is a rare occurrence on those Days. Supposing that my impression is right, can the annual Day-long slump in lethal activity be ascribed to superstition, stupefaction, a seeping into the most ill-natured of the Spirit of Goodwill? Any or all of those constraints? Others? Surely religious fervour, as opposed to simple and sensible religiousness, is not one of the constraints, for such fervour — one of the most forbidding kinds of madness, one of the mainsprings of murder in thought-to-be-good causes — seems to be affected more by phases of the moon than by dates on the calendar.

Despite the dreariness, criminously speaking, of Christmas Days, the encompassing Festive Seasons — each dating uncertainly from when greetings cards start arriving till Twelfth Night — are bountiful of murder cases that deserve to be recorded.

Or used to be.

Most present-day murderers give murder a bad name. And nowadays (because the jury system has been turned into a black joke by the elongation of trials to the financial benefit of lawyers, and by the consequent evasion of jury service by nearly all those who have something worth while to do with their time), heinous killers, when prosecuted, stand an excellent chance of walking free — if not at once, having been acquitted of their killings, then within an inappropriately short while, their peers having been flummoxed into deciding that they were only manslaughterers: sufferers, like themselves, from diminished responsibility. And ever since the fitting punishment for the crime was abolished by politicians whose intentness on bragging of their "moral convictions" regarding "the sanctity of life" quite took their minds away from the need to replace hanging with an especial, longer-running punishment, murder has lost its premier position in the catalogue of misdeeds, thus making De Quincey's satire almost real:

> If once a man indulges himself in murder, very soon he comes to think little of robbing. And from robbing he comes next to drinking and Sabbath-breaking. And from that to incivility and procrastination. Once begin upon this downward path, you never know where you are to stop. Many a man has dated his ruin from some murder or other that perhaps he thought little of at the time.

And so the Christmas Murders gathered herein are of the old-fashioned sort. Chiefly from negative causes, they evoke nostalgia. None of them was done by a deprived dweller in an inner-city or by a member of a gang of psychopaths nationalistic on behalf of some other land; none of the accused persons had the cheek to claim a euthenasiacal motive for getting rid of an unloved one; none of the culprits was moved to murder by the effect of or need for drugs. All but one of the tales can be read as if they were inventions — which some of them, tempting plot-forlorn writers of fiction, have been made to seem to be; but elsewhere.

Though the collection is presented in two unsignified parts — murders committed shortly before Christmas Day, murders committed shortly after — the cases of each part do not come in calendar-chronological order but are in a sequence to the benefit of those people who, no matter what kind of book they read, save the dictionarial sort, stick to the advice of Lewis Carroll's King: "Begin at the beginning, and go on till you come to the end: then stop."

Jonathan Goodman

The Christmas Sack Murder

Richard Whittington-Egan

A MERRY CHRISTMAS to you.

If, at the festive season of the year, when the pre-lunch sherry tastes sweet — or dry — upon your palate, and the brown and sizzling image of the turkey hovers on the near horizon, I were to invite you to play with me the old word-association game, I would hazard that the word *sack* would bring to your mind a vision of that cornucopian bag slung traditionally over the broad, red shoulders of that beamingly benevolent, white-whiskered old gentleman, Santa Claus. Or, possibly, if the children are all grown up, and the stamp and patter of tiny feet no longer punctuate the pattern of your Yuletide, the word *sack* might ally itself in your mind to the word *dry* — and from this combination would flow the golden stream of a certain, and delectable, variety of sherry.

For myself, however — and no doubt the psychiatrists would draw some very sinister conclusions from this — I have only to hear the word sack, and the theatre that lies beneath the vaulted white dome of my skull is instantly set with a very different series of images.

It begins, this grisly charade within my head, in total darkness.

Then ... gradually ... out of the blackness grow glow-worm points of flickering light. They shape themselves into gas-lamps, and, in their fitful yellow radiance, I see a long, dark street.

Along this street something is moving.

It comes more closely into focus — a hand-cart. And, pushing it, two shadowy figures.

My vision "pans in", as the television people say, on to the hand-cart, and I see upon it a sack.

There is something about the contours of that sack that

9

shocks me. For a moment or two I am puzzled, then . . . suddenly. . . .

But let me begin my winter's night tale at the beginning, for the shades that haunt this Christmastide reverie are no mere marionettes of fantasy. They are the ghosts of flesh and blood, who moved about their nefarious business through the murk of a long-ago December night in Liverpool.

Let us turn back the leaves of the calendar. Back through other Christmases. Back beyond the anxious Decembers of the Second and the First World Wars. Back to the night of Wednesday, 10 December 1913.

It is a night of high wind. A full moon rides among the scudding clouds. A solitary figure is pacing slowly the deserted pavement of Old Hall Street. All around are locked, bolted and shuttered shops and offices. Tall, Dickensian stools stand forlorn in dark and empty counting-houses. Up and down the aeolian canyon of the wind-loud night street the patient sentinel moves.

He is Walter Musker Eaves, a young ship's steward on shore-leave from the *Empress of Britain*, and he has an appointment to meet his sweetheart, Miss Mary Catherine Shepherd.

She is exercising the lady's privilege of being late.

He glances at his watch.

Half-past seven.

An extra-violent gust of wind blusters up from the nearby River Mersey, sweeps along the narrow street and, with a clatter, clouts a wooden shutter from the frontage of a shop that Eaves is passing. It strikes him a glancing blow upon the head, denting the brand-new bowler he has proudly donned in honour of Miss Shepherd.

And, as he stands there, ruefully contemplating his damaged headgear, a boy emerges and picks up the shutter.

"Hey! Just a minute," shouts Eaves. "Your shutter's ruined my new hat."

Quick as a lizard, the boy darts back into the shop. Comes out again seconds later accompanied by a young man in a grey suit.

There is some conversation between Eaves and the young man in the grey suit. A reiterated complaint. An apology. Some talk of compensation. A florin is pressed into Eaves's hand. A cordial "Goodnight."

The boy and the young man step back into the shop. Eaves resumes his pacing.

Presently, he sees the shop-boy walking up the street, pushing a hand-cart. He is followed, several yards behind, by the young man in the grey suit.

They disappear in the direction of the Lock Fields . . . and the Leeds & Liverpool Canal. . . .

In the year 1913, the shop premises at Number 86 Old Hall Street were occupied by a Mr John Copeland Bradfield, a tarpaulin manufacturer, who also owned a factory in nearby Great Howard Street. Bradfield himself spent the greater part of his time at the works. The shop was managed for him by his forty-year-old spinster sister, Christina Catherine Bradfield.

Miss Bradfield exercised a sensible, no-nonsense dominion over a staff of three: Miss Margaret Venables, a typist; George Sumner, a twenty-two-year-old assistant-cum-packer; and an eighteen-year-old lad rejoicing in the somewhat ornamental name of Samuel Angeles Elltoft.

Although she was not exactly a tartar, Miss Bradfield was a conscientious woman, dedicated to her brother's interests, on the prim side (as befitted a Sunday School teacher), and scrupulous to see that her tiny staff worked as hard and honestly as she did.

The hours of business were from half-past eight to six o'clock, and Miss Bradfield was always the first to arrive and the last to leave.

At ten minutes past six on the evening of 10 December 1913, amidst the clutter of rope and twine and piles of horse-cloths and sacks, Miss Venables puts on her hat, coat and mittens. She is hurrying because she has a train to catch. Miss Bradfield is counting the day's takings. Sumner is sweeping. And Elltoft is putting up the shutters.

What was done behind those shutters in that dimly lit shop after Miss Venables had gone home was sheer *grand guignol*.

11

Miss Christina Bradfield

Had Miss Bradfield, one wonders, any inkling, any fleeting clue, as she sat there beneath the gas-jet, ranging the sovereigns, the half-sovereigns, the silver and the copper in neat piles, of the awful thing that hovered in the air of that dusky, old-fashioned shop?

Did she, perhaps, glancing up as she shovelled the money — seven pounds and one penny — into the little leather satchel which it was her custom to take home each night to her lodgings over the water in Tranmere, see the glittering eye of George Sumner fixed upon her?

Or was it, when he pounced, a total and terrifying surprise?

Imagine — if you can bear to — the split-second of horror, the unspeakable terror, that must have gripped her as she saw

George Ball, alias Sumner

that young man over whom she had ruled with kindly severity for four years eight months, change without warning into a different, an utterly menacing, creature.

It was as if the docile shop-cat had, by some nightmare magic, been transformed into a ravening tiger.

The sudden and terrible unfamiliarity of the familiar must have nearly stopped her heart.

With ferocious bestiality, this "quiet" young man fell upon her. He clawed the clothes from her back, humiliated her, assaulted her, and, in a frenzy that surely slipped temporarily over the border of sanity, beat her to death with a rope-splicing fid.

It was only when the prim Miss Bradfield, half-nude,

trussed-up like an obscene, plucked chicken, had been reduced to a bloodied pulp that he came to his senses . . . and found himself standing athwart a corpse.

And where was young Elltoft while all of this was happening? We do not know for sure.

Nor do we know precisely how the labours of disposal — the cleaning-up, the packaging — were apportioned between the man, Sumner, and the boy, Elltoft.

All we do know is that the roped and doubled-up body was sewn into a sack (Elltoft was a dab-hand with a needle), laid upon the improvised hearse of a hand-cart, and trundled, half, three-quarters, of a mile through smiling moonlight and wind-rinsed streets.

Up Old Hall Street . . . turn right into Leeds Street . . . left into Pall Mall. The funeral route unwinds. Past lifeless warehouses, depots and manufactories. Not another living soul; not a single moving vehicle. The universe empty — save for themselves, their burden of meat, and a solitary starveling black cat streaking, startled by the rumble of their approach, under a railway arch.

Pall Mall narrows and becomes Love Lane — "Sugar Land", dominated and overshadowed by the towering bulk of Tate & Lyle's. Then Love Lane leads, straight as a die, to where, in 1913, the Lock Fields begin. And across the clinging clay of this stark and rubble-strewn stretch of industrial no-man's-land they bore the body of Miss Bradfield. There stand the locks. White-painted. Heavy brown timber gates. Slabbed stone basins filled with dark and brooding water. The moonlight boys tumble the corpse in its sackcloth shroud into the cold, wet grave of the Leeds & Liverpool Canal.

At five minutes to nine the following morning, when Miss Venables arrived, bright and neat, at the shop, she found Sumner and Elltoft already there, busily sweeping. But — unprecedented occurrence — of Miss Bradfield, the early-bird manageress, there was no sign.

When I met her, fifty-eight Decembers on, Miss Venables was an old lady of seventy-nine. I sat with her and her husband in the bright living-room of their home at Maghull, on the outer edges of Liverpool.

"When Miss Bradfield didn't come in that Thursday morning, I never in my wildest dreams thought that she had been murdered," she told me. "And I certainly didn't think that the boys had anything to do with her disappearance. I always liked George Sumner. He was a good-looking, polite, cheerful young man, and very keen on music. He used to lend me gramophone records. I found it hard to believe he was a murderer. Young Sammy Elltoft was a good boy, too. Very much under George's thumb, though. They were both so calm and collected that morning Miss Bradfield was missing, you'd never have guessed they were involved."

There was still no sign of her around eleven o'clock, when Mr Bradfield came into the shop in Old Hall Street. And to make matters even more mysterious, her landlady, Miss Holden, had telephoned from Tranmere. Miss Bradfield had not come home last night. Was she all right?

Hearing this, Mr Bradfield thought she might have gone to stay with her married sister, who lived in the suburb of Wavertree. He made enquiries. No, she had not seen Christina. Worried now, he got in touch with the police.

Meanwhile, shortly after midday, Francis Robinson, master of the barge *William*, was on the verge of picking the key to the mystery from the lock — No. 3 Lock of the Leeds & Liverpool Canal.

Arriving at the eastern end of No. 3 Lock, he had difficulty in opening the gates. He put his boat-hook down to investigate, and deftly hooked up the obstruction — a large waterlogged bundle. Then turned pale. Protruding from the dark and dripping sack was a black-stockinged leg.

Suspended, like an identity disk, by a thin silver chain around the neck of the female corpse was The Clue of the Three Monkeys.

Later that day, Mr Bradfield identified the body at the Prince's Dock Mortuary. So did Miss Holden.

Among other things, there could be no mistaking the little

At the Liverpool Police Court, Elltoft is on the left, Sumner, alias Ball, between the two constables.

silver medallion on the chain. It was a Japanese charm. The Three Wise Monkeys:

> *Swazaru* who speaks no evil;
> *Mizaru* who sees no evil;
> *Kikazaru* who hears no evil.

Miss Bradfield had always worn the lucky charm.

That night, or rather at half-past one on the morning of Friday, 12 December, the Liverpool police arrested young Elltoft. They found him sleeping peacefully in bed at his parents' house in Windermere Street, Anfield.

They went also to Sumner's lodgings, in Boundary Lane, West Derby Road. But that young gentleman had flown.

Throughout the next eight days, the greatest manhunt that had ever been seen on Merseyside was mounted. Christmas was still a week or so away, but distinctly gathering its festive shape out of the murk of the December dusk. In the bright-lit streets and shops, town-folk were packing their shopping bags and baskets with gaily-papered parcels. But while the people of Liverpool went merrily about their seasonal preparations,

16

anxious policemen, with no time and little inclination for festal frivolities, went grimly about their vital search for the killer.

They combed the gigantic warehouses around the docks, the seamen's boarding-houses, the seedy Sailortown pubs and cafés. On the Saturday, squads of detectives mingled with the Christmas shoppers — and the crowds at local football matches, for George Sumner was known to be mad about football. His photograph was shown on the screens of the city's "electric picture palaces".

Rumour, that lying jade, had it that he had stowed away aboard the *Majestic*, bound for New York. The vessel was searched at Queenstown, and, yet one more fantastic coincidence in this chance-riven saga, a steward was discovered aboard her whose name happened to be George Sumner.

Spurred by the offer of £50 reward, Liverpool became a city of peeled eyes and amateur detectives.

But of Sumner — or Ball, as the police had now discovered his real name to be — there was absolutely no trace.

Christmas was only five days away when — pure chance again — Ball (as we must now call him) was run to earth. It was an old schoolfellow who eventually spotted him in the street. Ball was disguised. He had shaved his thick eyebrows; had bought himself a pink eye-patch and a pair of cheap spectacles. But his friend knew George's distinctive shuffling gait. He followed him and saw him go into the Mersey Lodging House Company's establishment at 84 St James's Street, where, it transpired, he had been staying for a week. Then George's friend told a policeman.

In the lodging-house hall, just before midnight on Saturday, 20 December, his twenty-third birthday, George Ball, alias Sumner, was arrested. His first question to the constable who took him in charge was as to the result of that day's big football match. *Plus ça change. . . .*

The trial of Ball and Elltoft opened at St George's Hall, Liverpool, on 2 February 1914. Mr Gordon Hewart, KC (who was to become Lord Chief Justice of England), prosecuted.

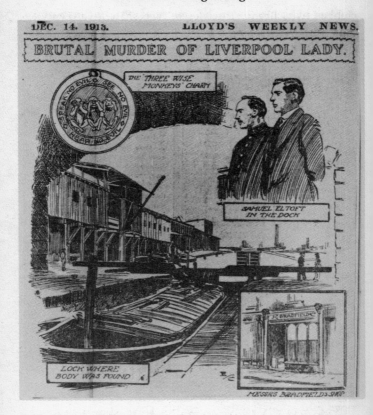

Ball was defended by Mr Alfred Tobin, who, four years before, had defended Dr Crippen.[1] Elltoft was represented by Mr Lindon Riley.

Ball's defence was a complicated cock-and-bull story about a man with a dark-brown moustache, who had suddenly materialized in the shop and held him at gun-point while he

1. See *The Crippen File* (Allison & Busby, 1985).

clubbed Miss Bradfield to death, then snatched her money-satchel before running off into the night.

Left with a corpse on their hands, he and Elltoft had, said Ball, panicked: they had decided that the only thing to do was to get rid of the body.

But when Elltoft went into the witness-box, he put paid to any faint chance that Ball might have had. The latter's story simply fell apart. It was a case of hanging together — or being hanged one by one.

"I was just leaving the shop at about seven or seven-fifteen," said Elltoft, "when George said, 'Stand outside. I won't be long.'

"I waited a quarter of an hour on the corner of Virginia Street. Then I went back to the shop. George came to the door. Just then a shutter fell. I put it up. Then George appeared with a hand-cart. I asked him what was in it, and he said a bag of rubbish. I wheeled it to the canal, and George dumped it. When I heard next morning of the disappearance of Miss Bradfield, I had not the slightest idea that anything was wrong."

But the jury did not have to rely upon these discrepancies alone. By any commonsense yardstick, the evidence against Ball was overwhelming. Accordingly, they brought in a verdict of Guilty.

So far as Elltoft was concerned, they felt that there was some measure of doubt — a doubt of which they decided to give him the benefit. He was found guilty of being an accessory after the fact, with the rider of a strong recommendation to mercy, and was sentenced to four years' penal servitude.

While Ball was waiting at Walton to be hanged, he made a full and frank confession of his guilt.

One of the things that weighted the balance in Elltoft's favour was the fact that not a shred of evidence could be adduced to show that he had in any way profited from the death of Miss Bradfield.

However, a detective subsequently examining Elltoft's bedroom had a sudden hunch. He unscrewed one of the brass knobs on the boy's bed — and there, nestling inside it, glinted two and a half gold sovereigns. The price of his co-operation?

Had the jury known about the cache, things might have gone very differently for young Sammy Elltoft.

That the money was discovered at all was pure chance. But so much in this extraordinary case boiled down to the workings of chance.

It was pure chance that that shutter blew down when it did, and fell on Walter Eaves's new hat. If it had not, Eaves very likely would not have noticed, and been able to identify beyond any reasonable doubt, the pair who pushed the hand-cart with its macabre load to the Lock Fields that night. And his evidence was vital.

It was pure chance that Christina Catherine Bradfield's body fouled the lock-gates and lay there awaiting discovery, instead of being swept out by the swirl of the waters into the Mersey, as Ball had calculated.

But Chance is a two-edged sword. While it saved the life of Samuel Angeles Elltoft, George Ball justly perished beneath its avenging blade.

If Sammy Elltoft is still alive, he will be an old man in his nineties. Surely, every Christmas of his life, he must remember that long, long ago Christmas when, but for his youth and a prodigal gift of luck, he might well himself have decorated not the Christmas, but the fatal gallows, tree.

The Ratcliffe Highway Horrors

Harold Furniss

> Go, hie thee, hie thee, from this slaughter-house,
> Lest thou increase the number of the dead.
> . . . A cockatrice hast been hatched to the world,
> Whose unavoided eye is murderous.
> SHAKESPEARE: Richard III, Act IV, Scene 1

TWICE IN ITS EVENTFUL HISTORY has the East End of London experienced a veritable reign of terror through the monstrous deeds of one man. In 1811 the horrors perpetrated in Ratcliffe Highway reduced that part of the Metropolis almost to a state of siege; and history repeated itself in 1888, when a fiend in human shape roamed about its narrow courts and alleys, scattering ruin and terror wherever he was drawn by his lust for blood. The alarm occasioned by the wholesale butcheries which terrorized the East End in the early part of the last century pervaded all classes, and reference to the dread affairs is found in many of the best literary productions of that time. Mention of the murders is to be found in the letters of Charles Lamb, and other celebrated authors of the period testified to the terror inspired by them in all grades of society. Many wealthy families fled from London as from a place of pestilence, and only a widespread rumour — heaven knows how arising — that the miscreant had gone to the provinces induced them to return.

Masters of households barricaded their doors and slept with loaded pistols beneath their pillows. Nervous women, whom circumstances compelled to live alone, refused to retire to rest at all, and sat up all night, talking with bated breath and fearful glance in threes and fours, for company. Hardly a window could be seen that did not exhibit a musket, a rattle, or a broadsword, that the mysterious miscreant, if he were passing that way, might see that the inmates had at hand the means of defence and the will to use them.

The watch was doubled and trebled, and, as in 1888, amateur detectives and self-appointed constables patrolled day and night the various streets in the East End. The horrible deeds were the actual cause of an invention. Doors were provided with chains at the foot, so that a cautious person summoned by knock or ring need not admit the intruder until he had taken full stock of his person and satisfied himself that the visitor was not a potential robber and murderer.

As I have said, much has been written concerning these affairs, and even in up-to-date literature one often comes across an account of them; but none of these are quite correct or authentic, and a description of them which shall be both cannot fail to be of interest and of value.

Even the great De Quincey, in his treatise entitled "On Murder Considered as One of the Fine Arts", does not give a perfectly accurate account of the horrors of 1811; although his version, from a literary point of view, is the finest description of a murder extant. The means of procuring the real and actual facts are difficult of access, and not to everyone's hand; but the reader who honours me with a perusal of these lines may rest assured that the following account contains nothing which is not true, and omits nothing which ought to be stated.

After those few preliminary comments, let me proceed with my plain, unvarnished history.

A hundred years ago, that part of London — the London of dark docks and dismal wharves, of foreign seamen and of land-sharks — now known as St George's-in-the-East, was called Ratcliffe Highway, and had been so designated for many years. It was not a pleasant neighbourhood, nor one in which the proverbial "wise man of the East" would venture with a gold chain and a diamond scarf-pin. Doubtful and dangerous characters abounded, and the foreign marauder here joined forces with the home-made article to such effect that the peaceful and law-abiding citizen usually gave "the Highway" the widest of berths. Still, even here, there was at least a leaven of respectability, and a few of the older and more permanent inhabitants and shop-keepers were sufficiently reputable. Amongst these "few righteous" was included, in 1811, Mr Marr, a young tradesman who kept a linen-draper's shop at No. 28 Ratcliffe Highway. Marr had at one time been to sea, but, coming in for a nice little property, he resolved to abandon his seafaring life, marry, and settle down, and he had not long been established in this shop when our story opens.

At that time his family consisted of his young wife, Cecilia Marr; a male child only a few weeks old; James Gohen, an apprentice boy; and Margaret Jewell, a young girl who was engaged as servant, and who was devoted to her kind master and mistress. Indeed, Mr and Mrs Marr were universally liked and well-spoken of by all their neighbours, and by everyone with whom they came into contact, the wife being very pleasant and pretty, and the husband industrious and agreeable.

Saturday, 7 December 1811, had been a very busy day with Mr Marr, who was kept abundantly employed by constant customers, and it was not until close upon midnight that he began to think of closing his premises. With this view, he and the shop-boy began to replace on the shelves the various bales of goods which he had been showing that evening to purchasers, and a little after twelve a watchman noticed him shutting up the shop windows. After this he told the girl Jewell to fetch some oysters for supper, giving her a one-pound note for that purpose, and she, leaving the outer door ajar, hurried to the shop of a Mr Taylor, but he had sold out and closed his shop, and so the girl endeavoured to procure the oysters elsewhere. To the fact of the first shop's being closed she undoubtedly owed the preservation of her own life.

On her way to another fish shop at John's Hill, she returned past Mr Marr's shop and noticed him through the window still behind the counter. She then proceeded to a baker's with the object of paying his account, but his shop was also closed, and, failing to find an oyster shop open, she returned again to her master's shop.

She had been gone about twenty minutes, and she was

rather surprised to find that the shop door was now securely fastened from the inside. A light within was visible, and she rang at the bell; no answer being forthcoming, she rang and knocked repeatedly, but to no effect. She thought, however, that she heard some person come upstairs while she stood at the door, and imagined it was her master coming to let her in. She also distinctly heard the feeble cry of the infant. At that dramatic moment there is no doubt the murderer was still within the house, but her repeated ringings alarmed him, and he made a hurried escape before it was possible to rob the house. There, however, the girl stood, ringing the bell again and again and kicking at the door until the watchman came along, calling the hour of one. He desired her to move on, not knowing her, and she explained that she was servant there and was locked out. He then remarked that Mr Marr had not locked the door, and he called out his name very loudly two or three times through the keyhole.

The noise attracted the attention of a Mr Murray, who lived next door, and he came out and enquired the cause of the disturbance. The matter being explained to him, Mr Murray went to the back of his own house, and from there observed that there was a strong light burning at the back of Marr's place. He then forced an entrance through the back, opened the street door, and admitted the girl and the watchman, who had now been joined by another of that not too intelligent fraternity.

The spectacle that confronted them can better be imagined than described, and the poor girl went into violent hysterics at the mere sight of such horrors, which, for a time, seemed to even petrify the men.

The first body seen was that of Mrs Marr, who was lying on her face, with all her clothes covered with blood and her feet towards the door, which at first prevented its being opened. She was quite dead, but not cold. Her head was frightfully fractured, the brains protruding on one side of her injured skull, and she lay in a deep pool of blood. Mr Marr was found behind the counter, with the marks of a tremendous blow on the head; his nose was broken in, the occipital bone also fractured, and the left eye showed traces of a violent blow. The boy Gohen had evidently made some resistance to the murderer, for he was fearfully mangled, having severe contusions on the forehead and nose, with the occipital bone dreadfully shattered and the brains protruding, together with other marks of violence about the body. The baby was found in its cradle, and its age rendered it impossible that it could ever have borne evidence against the ruthless slaughterer of its parents; yet the inhuman murderer had not hesitated to add this smiling innocent to his other victims. The child showed a large incision three inches in depth upon the left side of its throat, and its face on the same side bore several marks of frightful violence.

Such was the scene presented to the gaze of the first spectators of the monster's handiwork. The manner of the murders now seems clear enough. The villain had entered the shop and requested Mr Marr to show him some stockings, for which purpose the linen-draper had to turn round, with his back to the customer, and face the shelves above the counter. As he was removing a packet from the shelf, he received a tremendous blow with some heavy instrument on the back part of the head; and then another, the blow descending on his face as he turned to confront his assailant. The boy, possibly attempting to go to his master's assistance, was then seized, and struck in the same way. Mrs Marr was below in the kitchen with her baby on her lap, hushing it to sleep. The noise and scuffle — momentary as they were — brought her hurriedly upstairs, after placing the infant in the cradle, and she was seized by the bloodthirsty monster and instantly despatched with the same instrument as had killed her husband and the boy. The child, disturbed at being hurriedly laid down, commenced to cry, and the murderer descended and added another victim to the holocaust. Thus was the little household wiped out in the course of three or four minutes of time.

The first idea that struck the horrified spectators of this butchery was that the miscreant or miscreants might still be in the house engaged in robbery, and they opened the street door

HE RECEIVED A TREMENDOUS BLOW WITH SOME HEAVY INSTRUMENT.
(See our story of the Ratcliff Highway Horror)

Vol. V. No. 60.

again and gave an alarm. Late as it was, a huge concourse soon gathered, and the utmost excitement prevailed when the nature of the tragedy became known. The nightly watch gathered together, and the drum beat to arms. So huge a crowd gradually collected that it became necessary to again close the door of the slaughter-house. It was soon made clear that the murderer had made his escape at the back of the house with little or no plunder. He had doubtless been alarmed by the continuing ringing of the servant. In the desk of the shop a sum of £152 was found deposited in a tin box, and no property had been taken from the upper part of the house.

On a thorough search being made, a ship-carpenter's maul, about 8lb. in weight, broken at the point, and a brickmaker's long ripping-chisel, about twenty inches in length, were found, the former of these two formidable instruments being covered with fresh blood. Appearances — such, for instance, as the fact of the weapons being found — induced a belief that two men were engaged on this atrocious crime, and it was stated at the time that the prints of feet of different sizes were observed in the mud at the back of the house. It is certain that the escape was made from a window at the rear of the premises, and the neighbourhood must have been well known to the miscreant, for otherwise he could not possibly have found his way. As it was, he found it necessary to throw down some palings and to pass along a narrow path between two fences made for privacy.

The funeral of Mr and Mrs Marr and their infant son took plac on Sunday, 15 December 1811, at St George's Church in the East, and was witnessed by an enormous assembly of people, who openly expressed their sympathy with the relations of the deceased, and their detestation of the murderer. Nothing, indeed, so infuriated the populace as the useless murder of the child, and threats as to what they would do if the villain was found were heard on all sides. The body of the unfortunate shop-boy was interred in the same burial ground by his own relatives.

On Tuesday, 10 December, the coroner's inquest was held, and the deepest interest was manifested in the proceedings.

The first witness was a Mr Salter, a surgeon in Ratcliffe Highway, who gave a technical description of the various injuries received by the deceased persons; and then Margaret Jewell, who was greatly affected, and whose evidence was interrupted by a fainting-fit, gave her testimony.

Mr John Murray, a pawnbroker, of 30 Ratcliffe Highway, deposed that about a quarter past twelve on the Sunday morning he was sitting at supper with his family, and he heard a noise in the next house — Mr Marr's — which appeared to come from the shop floor. It resembled, he said, the falling of a shutter or a chair, and he likewise heard the shrill cry of a boy or a woman, as if it proceeded from someone under the influence of a great fear. At a quarter to one he heard a violent ringing and knocking, which continued till 1.15, when he went out to see what was the matter. He clambered over a wall which separated Marr's house from his, and found the bodies weltering in their gore.

George Olney, a watchman, stated that Mr Murray suddenly opened the door and said, "For heaven's sake come in and see what dreadfil murder is here!" He gave a description of the state in which he found the bodies and then he produced the ship-carpenter's maul, which was seen — the sight sending a thrill of horror through the room — to be still covered with blood and hair.

At the close of the proceedings, the jury returned a verdict of "Wilful murder against some person or persons unknown".

While this investigation was proceeding, the premises were examined by the sheriffs of London and by all the magistrates; rewards were offered and associations for detecting the guilty persons solemnly formed, a nightly watch was kept up, several arrests were made, and suspicious persons were examined. The only available clue to the culprit was the murderous-looking maul, which had been found to bear the letters J.P. in dots, faintly marked on the crown; but some days were to elapse before the weapon could be identified.

In the meanwhile, rumour asserted that the unknown miscreant had fled from London and was ready to resume his

FIFTY POUNDS
REWARD.

Horrid Murder !!

WHEREAS,

The Dwelling House of Mr. **TIMOTHY MARR**, 29, Ratcliff Highway, Man's Mercer, was entered this morning between the hours of Twelve and Two o'Clock, by some persons unknown, when the said Mr. **MARR**, Mrs. **CELIA MARR**, his wife, **TIMOTHY** their **INFANT CHILD** in the cradle, and **JAMES BIGGS**, a servant lad, were all of them most inhumanly and barbarously Murdered !!

A Ship Carpenter's Pæn Maul, broken at the point, and a Bricklayer's long Iron Ripping Chissel about Twenty Inches in length, have been found upon the Premises, with the former of which it is supposed the Murder was committed. Any person having lost such articles, or any Dealer in Old Iron, who has lately Sold or missed such, are earnestly requested to give immediate Information.

The Churchwardens, Overseers, and Trustees, of the Parish of St. George Middlesex, do hereby offer a Reward of FIFTY POUNDS, for the Discovery and Apprehension of the Person or Persons who committed such Murder, to be paid on Conviction.

By Order of the Churchwardens, Overseers, and Trustees,

JOHN CLEMENT,
Ratcliff-highway,
SUNDAY, 8th, DECEMBER, 1811.

VESTRY CLERK.

SKIRVEN, Printer, Ratcliff Highway, London.

butcheries in the large provincial towns, and the alarm spread to the latter.

Terrible proof was now to be given that rumour lied and that the fiendish wielder of the maul was still in town. Not yet had he satisfied his appetite for blood — not yet was he surfeited with human gore. Once more did he venture out under cover of darkness, and, clad in his long and handsome coat, betake himself to the scene of his next exploit. Once more did he hide a murderous weapon beneath the folds of his ample coat and wait the moment to exterminate another family.

Ah, Mr Williamson! Mr Williamson! Little do you know that the sands of time are running out fast for you, that even now the monster is peering at you, his next victim, through the open door, and that in a few moments he will be inside, a tornado of bestial fury, whose very breath speaks murder and sudden death. . . .

A Mr Williamson at this time kept a public-house at 81 Gravel Lane — an inconsiderable distance from the scene of the late tragedy — bearing the sign of the King's Arms. He was a strong and vigorous old man, whose family consisted of his wife, his grand-daughter, a servant named Bridget Harrington, and a lodger named John Turner. Mr Williamson was much respected in the neighbourhood, and, rough as it was, he contrived to keep his house as respectably as the best in the vicinity. The rival gin-palaces kept open till half-past twelve, but it was his custom to close his house punctually at eleven, and he never permitted any drunkenness, gambling, or swearing on the premises.

On Thursday night, 19 December 1811, shortly after eleven o'clock, the neighbourhood of Gravel Lane was dreadfully alarmed by loud cries of murder, and crowds of persons, their minds still fixed on the late dreadful events, soon collected round the house whence the appalling sounds proceeded.

A man was then observed descending, almost in a state of nudity, by a line formed by stringing together two sheets, from an upper window of the King's Arms. He appeared to be in a state of the greatest terror, and on reaching the extremity of his frail rope he was still some eight feet from the ground. However, he was able to drop with safety into the arms of a watchman, and then he announced, in the greatest agitation, that "they were murdering the people in the house". "Marr's murderer — now at work," De Quincey makes him say; but his exact words were as I have given them.

A consultation was immediately held, and it was rapidly resolved that an entry should be forced into the house through the cellar flap. By this means a man named Ludgate, a butcher living in Ashwell's Buildings, was the first man to enter, and he was followed by a Mr Hawse and a constable. Mr Fox, who resided exactly opposite, went back to fetch his sword, and he entered with three or four other persons through the front door, which had now been forced open.

They were met by a spectacle as heart-rending as that which had been seen at Mr Marr's. The fore room was in darkness, but a light was burning on a table in the middle room, which was used as a kitchen, and there they came upon the body of Mrs Williamson. She was lying upon her face along the hearth, with her head towards the door and her throat cut from ear to ear. She was fully dressed, some keys and a box were lying by the side of her, and it appeared that her pockets, which were turned inside out, had been rifled. The servant, Bridget Harrington, was lying between the body of her mistress and the fireplace, with her throat cut, and the whole room was flowing with blood. Besides the throat wound, the servant had received a frightful blow on the head. Mr Williamson in the meanwhile had been found by those who had descended into the cellar. He was found with his throat cut, lying on his back, with his head on the cellar steps, and he had first been struck down by a tremendous stroke on the skull. The theory was that he had probably descended to draw some beer for a late customer, who was no other than the murderer. While he was gone, the latter assailed the old lady, and it was then that the servant gave a cry which alarmed the lodger lying in bed above. The two women were soon despatched, and then the assassin met Mr Williamson at the top of the cellar stairs and struck him down, afterwards descending to make doubly sure by cutting his throat.

A search of the premises was commenced immediately, and it became apparent that the villain had left by the back. The inside shutters of one of the back windows had been taken down, and the sash thrown up, while the sill was marked with blood, as with the print of a hand, and there was blood on the inside iron bar. It was a good drop to the ground, which was vacant land belonging to the Dock Company, but there had been plenty of rain recently, and the earth below the window was soft and holding.

It was a very dark night, and it would not be difficult for anyone who knew the neighbourhood to get clear away, although in a back room of the house next door a large company was just then assembled, singing songs and drinking beer, and none of those roisterers saw anyone escape from the back of the King's Arms.

An iron crow, much stained with blood, was found near the body of Mr Williamson. As in the former case, the midnight murderer brought his weapon with him and left it behind.

The little grand-daughter, a child named Stillwell, slept through all these horrors, and was found upstairs in bed and fast asleep by those who had forced an entrance. According to De Quincey, the lodger snatched her from the bed and lowered himself with the rescued child in his arms; but I am bound to correct this error, which makes out the lodger a greater hero than he deserves.

Mr Williamson was robbed of a watch and what loose change he had about him, but there is little doubt that, as in the previous case, the villain was disturbed before he could achieve his object, viz., robbing the house. The murders had been committed by a left-handed man, and this had also been the opinion of the doctors who were consulted in the case of the unfortunate Marrs.

On the first alarm being given — and these fresh horrors plunged all London in a perfect state of frenzy — a picquet of the Tower Hamlets Militia was called out, and, assisted by the panic-stricken inhabitants, volunteers, and the constables, made a most minute search in all possible quarters, going literally from house to house, but without finding any persons to whom more than the most transient and unsubstantiated suspicion could be affixed. The ground seemed to have swallowed this man of blood, and yet he was living close by the scenes of slaughter!

It may be mentioned here that Mr Williamson was about

fifty-six years of age, his wife about sixty, the servant about fifty, and the grand-daughter, Kitty Stillwell, about fourteen. The old man had probably made a great resistance, even after the blow which knocked him down the cellar steps, for he was a powerful man, and, in addition to his other injuries, one of his legs was broken, and his hands were severely cut.

The Government, aroused to action by these fresh outrages, announced a reward of £500 for the discovery of the murderers, and the parishes of Shadwell and Ratcliffe offered £210. Twenty guineas was also offered to any person who could prove the selling of the iron crowbar found on the premises, and all possible steps taken to trace the owner of this and the other weapons. It is recorded that an extraordinary search was made of labourers' houses in the vicinity of Epping Forest on the strength of some incoherent rumour, and expresses were sent to the seaports to stop all suspicious-looking persons. In addition to the rewards specified, a free pardon was promised to anyone, except the actual murderer, who could bring the criminal to justice, and the following handbill was freely circulated:

Thames Police Office, Wapping

Whereas it is most particularly necessary that any person who may possess any knowledge of the maul with which the barbarous murder in Ratcliffe Highway appears to have been committed, should come forward and make the same known, the magistrates have caused the same to be again described, and do most solemnly and urgently require that every person who may be enabled to give the slightest information respecting it do immediately acquaint the magistrates therewith. The maul may be seen by any such person on application at this office. The handle of the maul is twenty-three inches long; the head, from the extremity of the face to the pin end, is eight inches and a half, and it has a flaw in the face, and the pin end has been broken off in flakes; it is marked faintly with the letters "J.P." in dots on the crown, near the face, and appears to have been so marked with a coppering punch.

By Order of the Magistrates,
E.W. SYMONS, Chief Clerk

December 20, 1811.

About this time two persons were taken into custody on suspicion, one of whom was put back for a second examination. It was shortly afterwards found that this suspect could have had nothing to do with the crimes, and he was set at liberty.

At the coroner's inquest, the most interesting evidence was that of John Turner, a sawyer by trade, who was the person who escaped from Mr Williamson's house while the murders were being perpetrated, and his account of the fell night's work was listened to with breathless interest. He said that he had lodged in the house of Mr Williamson for about eight months. His room was the front garret, which was two floors from the ground floor. On the night of the tragedy he had got home about half-past ten, and when he entered the house, Mrs Williamson was standing at the front door, and she had followed him in. He found Mr Williamson sitting in his greatchair in the middle room, and the servant was in the back room, no one else being in the house that he saw. A man named Samuel Philips then came in, and after asking for a pint of beer, he told the landlord that there was a stout man with a very large coat on peering in at the inner glass door in the passage, and Mr Williamson, catching up a candlestick, said, "I'll see what he wants." He returned in a minute, saying, "I cannot see him; but if I did, I would send him where he would not like to be." Philips then went away with his beer, and a Mr Anderson came in, but did not stay above two or three minutes.

Shortly afterwards the servant raked out the fire and Turner went to bed, at which time Mrs Williamson, carrying a watch and a silver punch-ladle, followed him upstairs to her own room. He heard her close and lock the door and go downstairs again, and then he undressed and got into bed. He had not been there more than five minutes when he heard the front door banged violently to, and almost directly afterwards the servant called out, "We shall all be murdered!" two or three times. Then came the sound of two or three heavy blows, and shortly afterwards, as the listener was sitting up in bed, almost unable to move from fear and horror, he heard the landlord cry out, "I am a dead man!" About two minutes after, he got out of bed and listened at the door, which had no fastening, but could hear nothing. He then crept softly downstairs to the first floor, and from below heard the sound of three heavy sighs, and he then heard someone walk across the middle room of the first floor very lightly. The listener was then halfway down the last pair of stairs. Hardly conscious of his own imminent peril, he actually descended to the bottom, and, the door being a little ajar, peeped through the opening. A candle was burning on the table, and by it he saw the murderer!

He saw a man, apparently nearly six feet high, in a large, rough "Flushing coat", of a dark colour, which reached down to his heels. He was standing with his back towards the horror-struck Turner, and was bending over the body of Mrs Williamson, whose pockets he was rifling. The witness heard some money rattle, and then the apparition — if one may so term a sentient being — rose and opened his coat with his left hand and put his right hand to his breast, as if he had a pocket there. Turner never saw his face, and he saw no other man. He ran upstairs as silently and as quickly as he could, and at first thought of getting under the bed, but instead took the two sheets, fastened them to the bedpost, opened the window, and lowered himself down.

Mr George Fox gave evidence as to making an entry into the house, and described the position of the victims, and he told how he, Mr Mallet — the chief clerk of the Shadwell police — and two police officers had proceeded to search a great many houses in consequence of information that two persons of a suspicious character had rushed along Shadwell High Street.

Mr William Salter, a surgeon, described the mortal character of the injuries, and said that the throats of all the victims had been cut by a razor used with the left hand. Two girls declared that immediately after the discovery two men had run past them, one in a white, rough coat, and the other a short man.

The jury returned a verdict similar to that found in the case of the Marrs, and efforts were renewed to trace the savage being who had destroyed two households.

A full description of the blood-bespattered maul having appeared in all the London newspapers, it was not long before some information came to hand with regard to that instrument, and it may be said at once that it led to the apprehension of John Williams on suspicion of being concerned in these atrocities. His arrest was followed by the procuration of so much strong circumstantial evidence against him as completely to establish his guilt.

Some writers assert that he had accomplices, but I consider that the facts point to his having done his fearful work alone and unassisted. It will be remembered that the witness Turner saw only one man on that fearful night, and after Williams's death nothing was ever discovered to indicate that others were concerned in the barbarous deeds which his cunning planned and his hardihood carried out. No, on mature reflection I am with De Quincey in giving all the credit, or discredit, to the diabolical Williams alone.

This libel on human nature is believed to have been an Irishman, and was about twenty-eight years of age. Amongst other reports concerning him, it was said that he had been a sailor, and that he had once sailed in the same ship as poor Marr. Rumour credited him with having quarrelled with the latter while at sea, and attempted to make out that the murders of that family were prompted by motives of revenge. Williams was about five feet nine inches in height, not lame, as was reported, and of well-set-up figure. His features were comely and regular, and his mass of curly yellow hair rather attractive than otherwise. De Quincey records, on the testimony of one who was present at his first examination, that his appearance was marred by his eyes, which were covered with a sort of film, which gave them a lack-lustre and fish-like appearance. On the same evidence he describes him as ghastly pale, and his hair as of a colour resembling the bright yellow of an orange. That he had good manners, and a most pleasant and insinuating address, is quite certain, and he seems to have been well liked by those who knew him. He had a passion for smart clothes, and the long surtout in which he did the murders was lined with satin. Previous to the crimes, he had worn long, sandy whiskers, but in the police office he appeared clean-shaven, and evidence was given that he had recently had them cut off.

He was a man of irregular habits, and at the time of his apprehension had no employment. Suspicion attached to him under the following circumstances.

It was known that he was a regular caller at Williamson's house, and he had been seen hanging about there at seven o'clock on the evening of the murder; nor did he return to his lodging at the Pear Tree public house in Sir William Warren's Square until very late on that particular night. A fellow lodger, a foreign seaman, was sitting up reading in bed, and Williams, on his return, very surlily requested him to put out the candle. On the evening preceding the last murders, he had borrowed sixpence from his landlady, but when he was taken into custody he had a good deal of silver, and on his person was found a pawnbroker's duplicate for two pairs of shoes pledged for 8s., £1. 14s. 0d. in silver, and a one-pound note. The magistrates ordered the publication of the marks on the note, for the purpose that any person having had such a note or who could at all trace the private marks might come forward and supply every information thereon.

One.
Bank of England, 1811.
No.16,755. Pay to Mr Henry Hase, No.16,755
on demand, the sum of One Pound.

269.
— Goodwin.

One.
1811, Aug. 23, London, 23 Aug., 1811.
For the Gov. and Comp.

£One

of the Bank of England.

T. Froggatt.

And endorsed on the back of the note:

Golding to J.D. — 7.12.11.

To account for these suspicious circumstances, Williams admitted that he had been at the King's Arms on the Thursday evening, and at various other times. He added that he knew Mr and Mrs Williamson very well, was quite intimate there, and that on Thursday evening when he was talking to the old lady she was very cheerful, and that she patted his cheek when she brought him some liquor. He gave an account of his subsequent movements, the truth of which does not appear to have been ascertained, and he explained that his only motive for desiring his bedroom companion to put out his candle was a fear of fire. For the money in his possession he accounted by describing it as the proceeds of certain pledging operations. After this statement, he was remanded for further examination.

In the meanwhile, a Mr Vermilloe, at whose house the prisoner lodged, declared that he could give some information respecting the much-advertised maul. Accordingly, that weapon was taken by the magistrate to Newgate, where Vermilloe was then confined for some trifling offence, and was immediately identified by him as one of a quantity of tools which had been left in his custody by one John Peterson, who was by trade a ship's carpenter, and was now at sea. That Williams had access to these tools was certain, and as a weapon exactly like this one was missing from Mr Vermilloe's house, it was fair to assume that it had been borrowed for the purpose of destroying life by the murderer.

It may be wondered why the man John Turner did not at once come forward and identify the prisoner if he were indeed the midnight assassin he had seen at work; but when, at Williams's next examination, the former gave his evidence, he was unable to swear positively that he was the man he had seen. It will be remembered, however, that he had not seen the murderer's face, and though Williams was known to him as a customer at the King's Arms, he could not swear to him by his figure and the long coat alone. He stated that while going downstairs he heard a man slowly walking in the sitting-room, and that his shoes creaked. This was at least curious, for a new pair of shoes worn by the prisoner creaked just in the same manner, and it may be stated here that the prisoner was left-handed.

Mrs Rice, a laundress, residing in Union Street, Shadwell, stated that she was sister-in-law to Mrs Vermilloe, and that she had washed for the prisoner off and on for about three years, and knew his stock of linen, which was of good quality. The magistrate rigidly examined this witness as follows:

Question: Have you not seen blood on his shirts?
Answer: Yes, I have; on one of them.
Q.: Have you seen any blood on his shirts since last Saturday week?
A.: Yes, I have; one of his shirts was bloody about the collar, like the mark of two fingers.
Q.: Was there no other part stained?
A.: I took no particular notice; the shirt was torn at the breast.
Q.: Will you swear there were no other marks of blood?
A.: There was a little blood on the arms, and several spots on parts of the body of the shirt. I kept it in order to mend it.
Q.: What linen have you generally washed for the prisoner?
A.: Four linen shirts and some stockings; but never any white handkerchiefs.

Mrs Vermilloe, the landlady of the Pear Tree, stated that she had known the prisoner for some time. There were two or three mauls in the chest of tools left with her husband by John Peterson, a Swede, who had gone abroad, and as the chest was never locked, anyone could handle or remove the weapons. Mrs Rice said that her two little boys used to play with a broken-pointed maul which was at their aunt's (Mrs Vermilloe's) house, and, as she thought they would know the weapon again, these boys were sent for. In the absence of the messenger, the prisoner said that he wished to explain how his shirt came to be torn and stained. At the Royal Oak Tavern he had been roughly handled by some Irish coal-heavers, and had had a scuffle with one who tore his shirt-collar and struck him a blow on the mouth, which cut his lip, and the blood from the wound stained his shirt. This was afterwards disproved by Miss Lawrence, daughter of the landlord of the Royal Oak, who said that she remembered Williams coming half-tipsy to the house, and there being some rough horse-play between him and some Irishmen, but she denied that any fighting took place, or that Williams's lip was cut in any manner at all. This occurred on a Friday, but the shirt had been found bloodstained the day before, and when this was pointed out to the prisoner, he said no more, and displayed some confusion.

Two fellow lodgers — Prussian sailors — of Williams's proved that the latter did not come home till close on one o'clock on the night that the Marrs were murdered, and that he undressed and went to bed in the dark. William Rice, a boy about eleven years of age, now arrived at the police office, and directly his attention was called to the maul he recognized it as the same he had frequently played with, though he had not seen it for some three weeks before then. The prisoner was then again remanded, and on the following Wednesday the magistrates went again to Newgate, and Mr Vermilloe positively identified the ripping-chisel found at Marr's house as one of Peterson's tools.

At a further examination of the prisoner — against whom the case now began to look very black — John Cuthperson, who also stayed at the Pear Tree, gave evidence. The substance of his statement was that on the morning after the last murders he saw a pair of his own stockings lying behind his chest, very much dirtied with fresh mud. He suspected Williams had used them, and asked that person if he had soiled his stockings in that fashion. "Why?" said Williams. "Are they yours?" Some little argument then arose as to the rightful ownership, and ultimately Williams washed them in the back-yard and returned them to the witness. Cuthperson added that the prisoner had recently been wearing a pair of light shoes which creaked a good deal.

About this time, John Frederick Richterson, a Dane, was believed to be an accomplice of Williams, and he was brought before the magistrates. He had lodged in the same house as Williams for about twelve weeks, but asserted that he knew little about him, except as a fellow lodger. A pair of blue trousers had been found under this man's bed in a damp state, and still bearing the traces of mud, this being the only circumstance of suspicion that could be alleged against him, and he declared that he had never washed the trousers, and did not know how any mud could have got on them. He went on to state that it was nearly half-past one when Williams returned on the night of Marr's murder, and the next day he went, from curiosity, to examine the bodies, but he did not tell Williams on his return where he had been. He said the maul resembled one he had seen at the Pear Tree, but he could not swear to it. He gave his evidence with much apparent reluctance. He added, however, with a queer glance at Williams, that he had heard a captain of a vessel with whom the former had sailed say that if ever he, Williams, went on shore again, he would certainly be hanged. This Dane was soon discharged.

A Mrs Hoare, who kept a chandler's shop next door to the Pear Tree, deposed that on the Saturday before the first murders, about half-past one in the morning, she heard a noise as if someone was attempting to break into the house, and, being frightened, she asked who was there. A voice, which she recognized as that of the prisoner, answered, "I am a robber," but she had no fear of him, and replied, "Whether you are a robber or not, I will let you in, and am glad to see you." Williams then entered, and proceeded to ask many questions as to how many rooms there were in her house, and the situation of her back premises, from which it may be surmised that he purposed one of his pleasant little night excursions in this direction. A chisel — stolen from Peterson's chest — was picked up by the watchman outside her window, and Williams remarked, "Whoever owned this chisel never intended you any good." One cannot doubt that he had dropped the chisel himself, and that but for his arrest Mrs Hoare would have been his next victim.

Williams was then again remanded, and the magistrate, addressing him, said, "You will be brought up again on Friday next." It is recorded that the prisoner gave a ghastly smile, and said, "Yes, if I am able to come."

On the Friday following, an immense number of persons assembled at the Shadwell Police Office for the purpose of witnessing the further examination of or getting a glimpse at the ruffian, whose guilt was now questioned by none. While all were awaiting in anxious expectation the arrival of the prisoner from Coldbath Fields Prison, the officers who had been despatched to bring him before the magistrates returned with the intelligence that they had found him hanging to a cross-bar six feet from the ground and extending along the ceiling, placed for the accommodation of prisoners to hang their clothes on. He was suspended to the bar by his white neckerchief, tied tightly round his neck; his body was quite cold, and he had apparently struggled hard. It is related that his face wore a cadaverous grin, as though in grim exultation at the thought of cheating the official gallows and of improvising a little execution of his own.

Though the man was dead, every scrap of information that could throw light upon the murders was eagerly collected, and the various witnesses were closely examined as to their knowledge of the suicide and his line of conduct.

Mrs Hoare related how the suicide-murderer used to visit her very often, nursing her young child and chaffing her daughter.

"Would you be frightened," he asked the latter once, "if you woke up one night and saw me standing by your bedside?" And the girl replied in all innocence, "No, if it were you, Mr Williams, I should not."

But other people felt less confidence in this extraordinary man, who seems to have inspired the utmost distrust and dislike in some people and the greatest liking in others. Thus Mr Lawrence, landlord of the Royal Oak public-house, informed the magistrates that he had several times requested Williams to keep away from his place, and Miss Lawrence, his daughter, had also objected to the familiarity with which he used to come into the house and sit in the bar.

Mrs Vermilloe related that on one occasion she had called him Williams to one of his friends, and the latter remarked that his name was John Murphy, not Williams, and that he was a native of Bandon, in Ireland. The first time she saw him was on the return from abroad of the *Dover Castle*, East Indiaman,

John Williams, drawn by Sir Thomas Lawrence soon after he was cut down

when he came home on that vessel and took up his lodging in her house. Afterwards he went on a voyage in the *Roxburgh Castle*, and had been home about twelve weeks when the Marrs were murdered. She never had any suspicion that the man was concerned in the atrocities until the maul and some stockings of his, mud- and blood-stained, were produced, and then she was afraid to turn him out of the house, as, if he guessed she suspected him, he might, she thought, murder her. He was a man of the most insinuating manners, she said, and made remarkably free wherever he went, entering into any and every conversation, and forcing his talk upon perfect strangers. If ever reference was made to the murders in his presence, he would walk into the passage, as if the subject of conversation was one he wished to avoid. She added that the only person who called on her respecting Williams after his arrest was a man named Fowler, who said he would "soon be cleared".

John Harrison, a sailmaker, and a fellow lodger of the defunct Williams, also gave evidence, and stated that he had seen Williams in company with a carpenter named Hart, who, by the way, had been engaged on some work in Mr Marr's house shortly before the murders. On the morning after the first tragedy he told Williams what had happened — that all Marr's family had been killed — and the former replied, "I know it." As he had not been out that morning, and, indeed, was still in bed, it is difficult to see how he could have learnt the news unless he had overheard Harrison telling Mrs Vermilloe. The witness said he suspected Williams from the first; at any rate, since finding the muddy stockings behind his bed. One day, as he and Williams were walking in the City, the latter said that he believed that Mr Marr had money to a considerable amount.

He said that, after the murders, he had often tried to search Williams's clothes for some marks of blood, but he was always baffled in these attempts, for whenever he attempted to approach the suspected man's bed, he seemed to suddenly waken. He was very restless, and much agitated at night, his sleep disturbed, and the witness often heard him talking in his sleep. One night, since the murders, he heard him say, "Five shillings in my pocket; my pocket's full of silver," and he did not reply when he (Harrison) called out to him.

Mr Lee, of the Black Horse Tavern, also related some more or less amiable peculiarities of this *grand monarque* of murder. He stated that he had seen Williams push against his wife and shake her pocket, as if to ascertain whether she carried any money, and on one occasion he caught him with his hand in the till, when Williams explained that he only wanted to get a halfpenny.

Harrison, the sailmaker, underwent a second examination in reference to a new French knife he had seen in the possession of Williams; it had a white ivory handle and a narrow blade.

The witness, after the latter's arrest, searched every part of the Pear Tree with a view to finding this knife, with which, in spite of Mr Salter's opinion that the throat-cutting had been done with a razor, there can be no doubt Williams had made sure of the deaths of his victims.

At last, the necessary at the back of Mrs Vermilloe's house was emptied, and rigidly examined, and herein an old pair of blue trousers was found; but it was not until 12 January 1812 that the knife was found. On that day Harrison, in searching amongst some old clothes, found a blue jacket, which he immediately recognized as having belonged to Williams. The inside pocket was quite stiff with coagulated blood, as if a blood-stained hand had been thrust into it and, without a doubt, this had been worn by the murderer when engaged on his deadly work. It was handed to the Shadwell police authorities, who at once sent down two officers to make further search in the house. In about an hour and a half the searchers came to a small closet, in one corner of which there was a heap of dirty stockings and other garments, and, on these being removed, they observed a mouse-hole in the wall, from which a piece of wood was protruding. This they drew out, and they then discovered the identical French knife, which was absolutely encrusted with blood, and which Williams must have hidden after the murders.

Meanwhile, at a coroner's inquest on the suicide, the jury brought in a verdict of *felo de se*, and it was arranged that the burial of the body should take place publicly, at four cross-roads, with every possible mark of ignominy, to show the general detestation of the monster's crimes.

At ten o'clock on the night of Monday, 30 December 1811, Mr Robinson, the High Constable of St George's, and several other high officials, went to the prison of Coldbath Fields, and demanded the body. Being delivered to them, it was placed in a hackney-coach, and driven to the watch-house of St George's known by the name of the Roundabout, at the bottom of Ship Alley in Ratcliffe Highway. There the remains were deposited for the night, and on Tuesday morning, the 31st, they were placed on a platform, erected six feet above a very high cart, drawn by one horse. The platform was composed of rough deals fastened together, raised considerably at the head, and thus the corpse was elevated, the face being turned towards the horse.

The body wore a clean white shirt, open at the neck, and neatly frilled; the hair was combed, and the face had been recently washed. The countenance, it is said, looked healthful and ruddy; but the hands and the lower part of the arms were of a deep purple, and nearly black — presumably the results of strangulation. The lower part of the body was covered with a pair of clean blue trousers — the villain had affected blue attire — and brown worsted stockings, but his shoes had been removed. On his right leg he still wore a heavy iron. The fatal maul was placed by the right side of his head and the ripping-chisel or crowbar on the other side, the whole forming a very weird spectacle. About ten o'clock, the procession — attended by the Head Constable and many other authorities on horseback, and about three hundred extra constables, with drawn cutlasses — began to move, and at a very slow pace approached the house of the late Mr Marr, where it stopped for half an hour. By the motion of the cart, Williams's face had been turned to the side, looking away from the house; but someone ascended the platform and placed the face in a position facing the scene of the first murders.

The procession presently wound its way down Old Gravel Lane by Wapping Wall, and at last came to the King's Arms, where again it remained stationary for a quarter of an hour. It then proceeded to Cannon Street, and, on reaching the top, where the New Road crossed and the Cannon Street Road began, it stopped again. A hole had been dug in the ground at this spot, and after a dramatic pause of ten minutes, the wretch's body was thrown into this unhallowed grave, amidst the acclamations of an enormous crowd.

A stake was now driven through the body, in accordance with the old rule regarding self-murderers, then the grave was rapidly filled with quicklime, and all was over. The actual burial was conducted in almost a complete silence, the solemnity of the occasion and the fearful nature of the dead

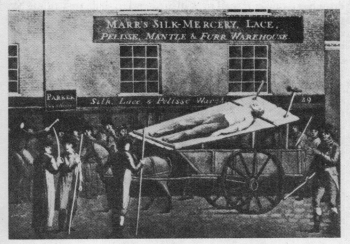

"Ignominious exposure of the Body of that inhuman Murderer, John Williams. . . ."

man's offences appearing to awe and subdue even an East-end multitude. The huge crowds then dispersed in the most orderly way, and the maul and crowbar were taken back to the Shadwell Police Office, and are in the possession of the authorities and to be seen to this day.

John Williams was buried close to the turnpike-gate in the Cannon Street Road. In the year 1849 certain alterations and incidental road-mending had to be done in that vicinity, and at that exact spot a skeleton, with a stake driven through it, was unearthed. The find caused a great deal of comment, and revived interest in the fearful murders of thirty-eight years previously; for the authorities caused it to be announced that the skeleton was that of John Williams.

Whether or no the latter had accomplices will never be known, and must always remain a question. The witness Turner saw and heard only one man, and all the weapons with which the deeds were done — the maul, the knife, and the crowbar — were traced to Williams and to Williams alone. No one else was ever after arrested on suspicion of having been concerned with him, and no one ever came forward to volunteer any fresh information. The public was satisfied that the prime mover at least had been accounted for, and the minds of men became easy again.

Packaged Death

Albert Borowitz

WHEN THE END of the Spanish-American War was marked by the signing of a peace treaty in Paris on the evening of 10 December 1898, New Yorkers were free to enjoy the Christmas season with special gusto, and even the first lady, Mrs McKinley, rushed up from Washington to do her shopping. The great stores of the metropolis beckoned their customers to view the treasures they had heaped up for the holiday celebrations. R.H. Macy's advertised: "The store is like a colossal Christmas tree. Each aisle is radiant with hundreds of tokens and emblems of the festive season. Fixtures and counters are decked with the brilliant regalia of holiday merchandise. The displays appeal to your sentiment and thrift." The Barrios Diamond Co. at Broadway and Canal Street announced with becoming modesty "the greatest sale of jewelry in the history of the world". 24 December was proclaimed by the Wanamaker Company as the "Day of Things Forgotten", and the department store vowed its readiness to assist "that energetic personage, the Eleventh-Hour Buyer". A quieter voice arose from Union Square: Tiffany & Co. gave notice of the arrival of many new creations in gold and silver from their own workshops and "by intelligent selection of choicest European novelties direct from the principal manufacturers abroad".

The city's theatres and museums offered attractions that rivalled the lures of its emporia. On 6 December Marcella Sembrich made her first appearance of the season at the Metropolitan Opera as Violetta in *La Traviata*, and May Irwin's new musical comedy garnered the laughter that New Yorkers had lavished the month before on Weber and Fields's parody, *Cyranose de Bric-à-Brac*. The British influence made itself felt with *The Geisha* at the Harlem Opera House and

Trelawny of the Wells at the Lyceum. On Christmas Day, the fiftieth performance of *The Merchant of Venice* was on the boards at Daly's Theatre. For art lovers, the American Art Galleries, Madison Square South, offered an exhibition of the paintings of James Tissot, admission 50 cents on weekdays and 25 cents on Sundays.

The local news during the weeks before Christmas piqued the New Yorkers' love for scandal while leaving their holiday spirits undisturbed. In late November Commissioner of Correction Francis J. Lantry announced that the plans for the new Tombs prison were defective and that the beams and girders of the building would have to be strengthened at a probable cost of $20,000. It was the city's law courts, though, that provided the spiciest gossip of the season. Mrs Margaret E. Cody went on trial for attempted blackmail of the heirs of robber-baron Jay Gould through threats to disclose that Gould had fathered an illegitimate daughter. Despite the testimony of handwriting expert David Carvalho that Gould's name on the baptismal record of his reputed child had been clumsily forged, the jury could not agree on a verdict, with seven standing for conviction and five for acquittal. Even more intriguing was the series of trials that proceeded in December in the courtroom of Recorder John W. Goff. William Moore and his wife were separately tried for perpetrating a classic "badger game" crime at the expense of Martin Mahon, proprietor of the New Amsterdam Hotel. By prearrangement with his wife, Moore discovered her in the embraces of Mahon, and allegedly proceeded to rob him and force him at gunpoint to sign $5,000 in promissory notes. Mr Moore was convicted in a second trial after the first jury deadlocked; the jury in his wife's case was dismissed after fruitless deliberations for twenty-two hours. On 27 December, William Moore was sentenced to nineteen years after the district attorney told Recorder Goff:

> This crime has been known as the "badger" game since the days of Queen Anne. It is a diabolical crime, and because of its insidious nature there have been few convictions for it. It is one of the most dangerous that infests our community.

At the very moment that the district attorney was indulging in this hyperbole, a much more dangerous and insidious crime had been set in motion by an unknown criminal, a man who may have read one of Tiffany's discreet advertisements and decided that a silver object purportedly bought at that prestigious establishment would be just the right Christmas gift for an intended victim.

The case began on the day before Christmas. That morning Harry Cornish, the athletic director of the Knickerbocker Athletic Club, at 45th Street and Madison Avenue, received in his mail at the club a pale-blue box of the kind used by Tiffany's, wrapped in manila paper and containing a silver toothpick-holder shaped like a candlestick, about two inches in diameter and of the same height, and a one-ounce blue bottle of Bromo Seltzer. When Cornish removed the bottle

The Knickerbocker Athletic Club

from its paper wrapper, he found that it could fit into the holder. A small envelope was enclosed in the box, but the sender's card was omitted, as if by accident.

The "gift" appeared to be a playful caution against excessive drinking over the holidays. Cornish and his fellow club members had a good laugh over the waggish prank, and at his assistant's suggestion Cornish retrieved the manila wrapper from the wastebasket and cut off the address, in the hope that he ultimately might be able to recognize the handwriting. One clue he did not immediately notice: the misspelled number "Fourty" in the street address.

Cornish boarded uptown with his widowed aunt, Katherine Adams, and her daughter, Florence Rodgers. On 27 December, he brought his mysterious present home, much to the delight of Mrs Adams, who found that the pattern of the toothpick-holder closely matched the design of her silverware. Cornish's cousin Florence teased him with the remark, "Oh, some bashful girl has sent you a present." That night, the three went to a theatre, returning about midnight. The next morning, around nine o'clock, Mrs Adams awoke with a dreadful headache and called to her daughter. Remembering the bottle of Bromo in Harry's room, Florence immediately asked him for it. After drawing the cork of the bottle only with difficulty by the use of a dinner fork, Cornish poured out about a half-teaspoonful in a glass. He failed to observe in his haste that the grains of the powder were smaller than usual and effervesced only slightly.

As soon as Katherine Adams drank the mixture, she screamed and fell back on her bed, writhing in agony. Florence sent a hall boy for Dr Edwin Hitchcock, but only after a second call did the inarticulate messenger convince the physician of the seriousness of the situation. Hitchcock, with his stomach-pump and emergency bag in hand, ran to the Adams house but arrived to find Mrs Adams senseless. She lay on her back, her eyes rolled up and her jaw slack. The doctor administered restoratives but could detect only two very faint pulse beats. He told the frantic Florence and Harry who stood at the bedside that future efforts were useless. In fact, Mrs Adams had died within an hour of taking the draught.

Cornish, examining the glass from which his aunt had drunk, remarked that it could not be "dangerous" and took a small sip. His face immediately became livid and he retched uncontrollably. Dr Hitchcock, desperate for a remedy, instantly decided to test the deadly poison himself. He seized the bottle and poured as much on his finger "as might lie on a knife point" and placed it on the tip of his tongue. He instantly got a metallic taste and recognized the odour of almond, characteristic of cyanide. Beginning to become extremely nauseated, Hitchcock nursed himself with whiskey and shared a sour apple with Cornish. These homely cures appeared to work well, for both men soon began to feel better. Cornish, however, required several days' convalescence and medical attention.

Katherine Adams and Harry Cornish had both swallowed cyanide of mercury, which had been mixed with the white powder of Bromo Seltzer. Cornish could hardly be blamed for having failed to have his suspicions aroused by the painkiller package. Bromo Seltzer, then as now, was put up in a distinctive blue bottle. It was stoppered with cork to which a coating of paraffin was evenly applied. The bottle received by Cornish appeared at first glance to be properly sealed, but closer examination by the police showed that the label had been washed off a Bromo Seltzer bottle and pasted on a smaller one used by chemists for cyanide. The name Bromo Seltzer, blown into the drug firm's bottles, did not appear in the small bottle sent to Cornish. The paraffin veneer "was thick and irregular, as if pressed down hurriedly by human fingers".

The press corps lost no time in seeking out the close relatives of Harry Cornish, who had clearly been the poisoner's target. Who could have had a motive to murder him? His divorced wife Addie, interviewed in Boston where she lived with their ten-year-old daughter Jenny, was completely nonplussed and had no theory to offer. However, Cornish's father, Harry Cornish Sr., was apparently not tongue-tied when the new role of detective was thrust upon him; he was quoted as entertaining suspicions of a man and a woman. He said that his son Harry (then thirty-six) had had trouble with a man over a love affair when he was only nineteen years old. The press also reported professional speculations about the hidden murderer. Dr W.H. Birchmore, chemist and a recognized authority on cyanide, was convinced that "none but a physician of understanding, a pharmacist, above the average of such in chemical knowledge or a person not necessarily in either of these professions but well versed in chemistry, can be the poisoner in this case". Assistant district attorney McIntyre, questioned at the Democratic Club, limited himself to the observation that the handwriting on the poison package evidently had been disguised and looked as if it had been penned by a woman.

The bizarre murder stunned the public, for it was seen as a continuation of a recent wave of poisonings, many of them perpetrated by anonymous mailings. An early, widely publicized crime in this series was the 1891 murder of Josephine A. Barnaby, a wealthy Providence widow, by Thomas Thatcher Graves, a physician who had cured her of a paralytic disorder and abused her gratitude by obtaining control of her assets and by inducing her to appoint him executor and to grant him a large legacy. His instrument was a bottle of whisky containing a solution of arsenic strong enough to kill many widows. Pasted on the bottle was a written New Year's greeting asking her to accept "this fine old Whiskey" from her "friends in the woods", an intended allusion to an Adirondacks guide who was beginning to rival Graves as an object of Mrs Barnaby's beneficence. Mrs Barnaby died and her friend, Mrs Worrell, became ill after indulging in a toddy prepared from the "whiskey".

Perhaps the news of the Graves murder came under the eyes of San Francisco's celebrated poisoner, Cordelia Botkin, who gave a sinister new meaning to the culinary concept of "sweet and sour" by seeding with arsenic a box of candy she bought at a confectioner's store on Market Street. She mailed the box to Mary Dunning, the wife of her lover, who after a five-year liaison had had the poor taste to announce an intention of returning to his spouse.

Botkin cast her nets more widely than had Dr Graves, for although he might have expected his intended victim to share the poisoned whiskey with friends, the spurned Cordelia cunningly calculated that her gift would tempt the sweet teeth of the Dunning children. In the box of chocolates she had written in a hand unknown to Mrs Dunning: "Love to yourself and baby." As it turned out, the candy was eaten by four adults and two children and claimed the lives of both Mrs Dunning and her sister.

Botkin's trial began on 9 December 1898, less than three weeks before Mrs Adams drank the poisoned Bromo Seltzer.

In the meantime, two other murders by mail, apparently inspired by the Graves and Botkin killings, were reported in the press. On 12 November 1897, a man was murdered by poison contained in whiskey mailed to him as a gift, and on 9 September 1898, Margaret Wilkinson of Newark, New Jersey, was poisoned by a package of sugar mixed with arsenic.

The copycat murder syndrome was even more clearly in evidence in two successive New York City poisonings involving the administration of a painkiller.

In 1891 a young medical student at the New York College of Physicians and Surgeons, Carlyle Harris, under pressure to acknowledge publicly his secret marriage to Helen Potts, murdered her with a powerful dose of morphine. He had introduced the pure drug into a capsule that had originally contained a harmless sleeping draught consisting of quinine and a small quantity of morphine dispensed by a druggist on his prescription. Harris was tried in early 1892 and found guilty of murder.

In the course of the proceedings, the defendant received scant sympathy from another New York doctor, Robert W. Buchanan, who in conversations with friends referred to Harris contemptuously as an amateur and bungler because he had not known how to prevent the contraction of the eye pupil, which is one of the characteristic symptoms of morphine poisoning. Within a few months Dr Buchanan had occasion to follow precisely this formula for disguised

BARNET'S BODY IS EXHUMED IN BLINDING SNOWSTORM.

OFFICIALS WATCH THE RAISING OF THE COFFIN.

poisoning when he murdered his wife by the administration of a mixture of morphine and belladonna (atropine), the latter drug having dilative powers that forestalled contraction of the pupils. Although he had copied and improved on Harris's recent murder pattern, Buchanan was convicted like his predecessor, and both men were executed.

In the case of the Bromo Seltzer murder, the killer appeared to be imitating all these earlier crimes in the selection of a painkiller for his poison medium and in hitting upon an anonymous mailed gift as his means of delivery. But something even more alarming was soon observed at work: the Bromo Seltzer killer seemed to be copying himself.

This baffling likelihood surfaced early when a physician, Wendell C. Phillips, who attended Cornish after his poisoning, noted that his symptoms closely resembled those of another club member, Henry C. Barnet, who had died in the previous November after taking a dose of another patent medicine named "Kutnow powder", which he said had been mailed to him anonymously. Henry Douglass, Barnet's principal physician, submitted the medicine to a chemist for analysis and was advised that it contained cyanide of mercury, but because he attributed his patient's death to diphtheria, the damning chemical report was not called to the attention of the police until after the murder of Mrs Adams. The authorities then ordered Barnet's body exhumed, and the post-mortem examination confirmed the presence of cyanide of mercury.

The police investigation, with the able participation of Detective (later Deputy Inspector) Arthur A. Carey, hunted for a killer who must fit a unique profile. He must have had reason to desire the elimination of both Barnet and Cornish, two members of the Knickerbocker Club, and must also have had access to the uncommon poison, cyanide of mercury. Through the initiative of club members who thought they recognized the handwriting on the Bromo Seltzer mailing package, the attention of the police was drawn to a man who seemed to fill the bill precisely: a former club member named Roland B. Molineux.

Molineux, the thirty-one-year-old son of a Civil War

Roland Molineux

general, Edward Leslie Molineux, was a chemist and the superintendent of a Newark factory of Morris Herrmann & Company, a manufacturer of dry colours. The plant had a well equipped laboratory containing Prussian blue, chrome yellow, and other chemicals from which poison, including cyanide of mercury, could be produced. Rumours indicated that Molineux had strong, although varied, grievances against the two intended poison victims. Molineux and Barnet, it was said, had paid court to the same young woman, Blanche Chesebrough, who was regarded as a great beauty in spite of an artificial eye. When Barnet lay on what was to prove his deathbed, he received a letter from Blanche in which she expressed distress to learn of his illness and also assured him of her desire to see him to resolve some misunderstanding that had arisen between them. Seventeen days after Barnet's death, she married Molineux.

Although crime annals had taught that men murder for far less substantial reasons than those that impel them to commit lesser crimes, Molineux's grievances against Cornish (were Molineux indeed the sender of the Bromo Seltzer package)

Blanche Molineux before her marriage

would set a new standard in triviality. The police were told that Molineux had left the Knickerbocker for another athletic club after an unsuccessful campaign to have Cornish ousted from his post. Molineux's complaints had been many. Cornish had refused to follow his orders in connection with the club's plans for an amateur circus. And he had declined to order the make of horizontal bar preferred by Molineux, who was a champion gymnast and member of the club's athletic committee. He had written an insulting letter about a lawyer friend of Molineux, Bartow S. Weeks, asserting that Weeks was "guilty of a dirty piece of business". Still worse, Cornish had allowed strangers and athletic members to use obscene language in the club's swimming pool. Finally, it was said that, as Cornish was going downstairs from the room in which the club's board had rejected Molineux's complaints against him, he came upon his adversary. "You son of a bitch," he greeted Molineux, "you thought you would get me out and I got you out." Molineux resigned from the Knickerbocker Club in November 1897.

As the investigation proceeded, a strange pattern of

pre-murder conduct appeared to bind the two poisonings more closely together. Prior to the death of Barnet and the attempt on Cornish, fictitious letter-office accounts were established in the names of both intended victims; thereby, active correspondence was conducted in a disguised hand, ordering cures for impotence and other patent medicines. The medicines ordered from the "Barnet" letter-office box, established in late May 1898, included Kutnow powder; the renter of the box, whom the proprietor, Nicholas Heckmann, identified as Molineux, had called about twenty times to pick up his mail and packages. The "Cornish" box was rented on 21 December 1898, and a sample box of Kutnow powder ordered shortly thereafter by the false Cornish was delivered to the police by the letter-office proprietor in January. The personal information that was supplied in a "diagnosis blank" relating to a remedy applied for in the "Barnet" correspondence more accurately described Molineux than Barnet. The correspondence in both letter-office boxes contained many misspellings. In his memoirs, Detective Carey asserted that in samples of handwriting given by Molineux at the request of the police, he repeatedly spelled the word "forty" with a "u", as was done on the Bromo Seltzer mailing wrapper.

The police were also successful in tracing the contents of the lethal package mailed to Harry Cornish at the Knickerbocker Club. The toothpick holder had been sold by Hartdegen's jewellery store in Newark on 21 December; saleswoman Emma Miller remembered her customer as a man with a sandy Van Dyke beard who had asked for something to hold a bottle of Bromo Seltzer on a lady's dresser. (A number of Newark wigmakers conveniently told the press that they had sold red beards about the same date.) The bottle used by the poisoner was identified by a mark as originating with Powers & Weightman, manufacturing chemists.

Soon another important breakthrough was announced. At the inquest Molineux had denied ever having seen a letter in his ordinary hand on robin's-egg-blue paper with three overlapping silver crescents. That letter had been sent to Dr James Burns, asking for a medicine for impotence. The same stationery was used in correspondence through the fictitious letter-office boxes. It was now reported by the Newark police that Mary Melando, a fellow employee of Molineux at the Herrmann factory who took care of his rooms there, had seen sheets of similar paper in the drawer of his sideboard.

Mary told friends that Molineux had seduced her when she was thirteen years of age and that they had remained lovers until two years ago. Despite his abandonment of her in favour of Blanche, they still remained something of a mutual-aid team; she cleaned his rooms at the factory, and he had interceded in her behalf when she was caught in a police raid on a brothel. Full of gratitude, Mary refused to leave New Jersey to testify for the prosecution at the trial in New York City. Under the procedures of the day, she could not be compelled to cross the river. The means that were used to procure this essential witness for the state are worthy of James Bond. Detective Carey recalls the episode in his memoirs:

> She *did* testify, and in New York City. How she came to do this I shall not detail. Suffice it to say that she was fond of the theatre. She attended one in Paterson, New Jersey, one evening. She left the theatre after the performance in a great hurry and went to the railroad station. Two trains going in opposite directions pulled in. A man cried, "This train for Newark." Mary stepped aboard it. She discovered it was not going toward Newark but towards Suffern, New York. But the train had started. She got off at Suffern, and stepped into the arms of [Police Sergeant] McCafferty, who was waiting at the depot.

Indicted in July 1899 for murder in the first degree of Katherine Adams, Molineux went on trial on 4 December before the already-mentioned Recorder John W. Goff, presiding judge of the Court of General Sessions of the Peace. The redoubtable judge, ruddy-faced and white-bearded, has been described by Samuel Klaus, the editor of the trial volume, as "a convicting judge . . . who made up his mind as to the guilt or innocence of the accused; if he could not comment to the jury on the evidence, he used his discretion with liberality in favour of the side of justice as he saw it". Because of the barrage of pre-trial publicity, over five hundred talesmen had to be examined before a jury could be empanelled. The assistant attorney general, James W. Osborne, who was responsible for the state's case, faced this painfully selected jury with some reason for trepidation. Even though Recorder Goff might well be expected to favour the prosecution, Osborne was faced with the heavy burden of establishing guilt for the most secret of murders — poisoning — through the accumulation of circumstantial evidence. This burden was made more imposing in the Molineux trial by the physical remoteness achieved by the poisoner through the mailing of the lethal package. Osborne's grand strategy was to establish that the attempts on Barnet and Cornish were made in pursuance of a common design in which each murder was accomplished through the anonymous mailing of a package of patent medicine laced with cyanide of mercury and preceded by letter-office correspondence with remedy manufacturers in the forged name of the intended victim. Under this approach, evidence of the common authorship by Molineux of the Barnet and Cornish correspondence and of the address on the Bromo Seltzer mailing package would be a powerful means for bringing the whole scheme home to Molineux.

In following the prosecution plan, Osborne encountered a number of obstacles. After equivocating during direct examination [examination-in-chief], Emma Miller, the seller of the silver holder mailed with the Bromo Seltzer bottle, stated positively during recross-examination that Molineux was not the man she had waited on and that there was no possibility of her being mistaken. And although Nicholas Heckmann identified Molineux as having personally hired the letter-office box in Barnet's name, Joseph Koch, at whose office the Cornish account was later established, was equally sure that, while the defendant had called on him to talk about a letter-office box, a box ultimately was rented in Cornish's name by a "third man". The fiercest battle was fought over the authorship of the forged correspondence, with the prosecution offering fourteen expert witnesses, including two perennial handwriting analysts, John F. Tyrrell and Albert Osborn, who both reappeared in the Lindbergh kidnapping case thirty-five years later; the defence relied on the advice of another eminent authority on questioned documents, David Carvalho, who had in the previous year appeared for the prosecution in the trial of Margaret Cody for attempted blackmail of the Gould heirs.

On 6 February defence counsel Bartow S. Weeks, the same lawyer Cornish had maligned in the letter that had fuelled Molineux's anger, surprised the courtroom by declining either to offer evidence or to move for dismissal. He stated instead his belief that the prosecution had failed to establish its charge and immediately began his closing argument. When the jury returned after a day's deliberation, Weeks's confidence proved unfounded. The verdict was guilty.

Undaunted and against the advice of his lawyer, Molineux addressed the court before the death sentence was announced. He had not bought the bottle holder, hired the Cornish letter-office box, or possessed any of the instruments used in the crime. Nicholas Heckmann's testimony that he had opened the Barnet letter-office box was blamed on the sensation-seeking press: "Yellow journalism put a price upon my head. It was an invitation to every blackmailer, every perjurer, every rogue, every man without principle but with a price, and to that invitation Mr Heckmann responded." On 26 March 1900, Molineux was taken to Sing Sing prison.

In 1901 his appeal came before the New York Court of Appeals. The court unanimously reversed the conviction and ordered a new trial.

All seven judges agreed that the trial court had erroneously admitted hearsay testimony by Barnet's principal physician, Douglass, as to statements made to him by Barnet to the effect that Barnet had received the Kutnow powder through the mail and that he had become ill after taking a dose of it. Presumably Barnet's condition at the time of the alleged statements was not regarded as sufficiently hopeless for these crucial revelations to be regarded as "dying declarations". (Analogous hearsay evidence was admitted in the defence of Klaus von Bülow at his first trial, in 1982, for the attempted murder of his wife, when a hospital technician testified as to Mrs von Bülow's statement that she had tried to kill herself.)

On a broader issue of evidence that struck a devastating blow to the prosecution's case on retrial, the court split four to three. In a signal victory of common law over common sense, the majority held that admission of any evidence relating to the alleged killing of Barnet was barred by the general rule that "the state cannot prove against a defendant any crime not alleged in the indictment, either as a foundation for a separate punishment, or as aiding the proof that he is guilty of the crime charged". Holding that none of the recognized exceptions to that rule applied, the majority ruled, among other things, that evidence of the Barnet killing did not establish that the two murders were committed pursuant to "a common plan or scheme", nor did it tend to identify Molineux as the same person who committed the two crimes. In the majority's view, the use of cyanide of mercury in both cases no more established a common scheme than if the two victims had been shot — and indeed, the majority opinion noted, the widely differing motives put forward for the two crimes tended to disprove any connection.

The majority also discounted the significance of the letter-office box correspondence conducted in the names of the two intended victims, observing that this evidence showed merely that "if the same person was operating through both boxes, he was employing similar means for different ends, or for some common purpose not disclosed by this record. The methods referred to are as identical as any two shootings, stabbings or assaults, but no more so."

The principal dissenting opinion, written by Chief Justice Parker, appears to have by far the better of the arguments. The opinion noted that cyanide of mercury, the poison used in both killings, "is a rare and unusual poison, not kept on sale by druggists generally as strychnine and many other poisons are, and the books of the medical and chemical professions record only five cases, prior to these, of death by that poison". The fact that within a period of seven weeks two murder attempts had been made with this rare poison suggested the likelihood that one person had sent both packages. Parker also regarded the evidence of the correspondence carried on in the names of the two intended victims as relevant, not only because of the testimony by lay and expert witnesses that it was all in the handwriting of Molineux, but also because "there is to be gleaned from the letters themselves and the circumstances surrounding and attending their writing very strong evidence that one brain conceived and carried out both schemes". In each case the letter-office box was hired in the name of the intended victim; remedies for impotence were ordered in the victim's name; both the Cornish and Barnet letters were undated; and both series of letters, as well as the address on the poison package, contained misspelled words.

While the majority seemed troubled by the fact that the fictitious correspondence in the letter-office boxes had no rational connection with the ensuing murders, Chief Justice Parker clearly did not find it necessary to do more than note the highly unusual fact that the strange activity with reference to each intended victim preceded the mailing of the poison. Perhaps a more profound awareness of the irrationality often associated with criminal malice would have supported the view that the opening and use of the letter-office boxes in the names of Barnet and Cornish were hostile actions by which the would-be murderer appropriated the names and personalities of his intended victims before he made his attempts on their lives.

At the retrial, which began in October 1902, a number of factors swung the balance in Molineux's favour. First, of course, was the appeal court's ruling that evidence relating to the Barnet poisoning was inadmissible. Only six of the harmless Barnet letters were admitted as standards of comparison with the Cornish letters; the rest were excluded. Another advantage was that Mary Melando, having been tricked once by the police, could not again be enticed into an appearance in New York City.

But by far the most dramatic turnabout was the decision of the defence to put Molineux on the stand. Calm, smooth and convincing, he established an alibi for the afternoon on which the poison package was allegedly mailed at the General Post Office on Park Row — he was visiting a professor at Columbia University. He denied authorship of the Cornish and Barnet letters and maintained that he had never even heard of cyanide of mercury. He now admitted writing to Dr James Burns on the celebrated robin's-egg-blue paper but claimed that he must have picked up a sheet in some restaurant or hotel.

David Carvalho, never known to under-rate his own importance, subsequently cited as a major turning point a blunder by Osborne, the assistant district attorney, in his heckling cross-examination of Molineux. Osborne asked the defendant how he came to engage Carvalho, who had the reputation of testifying only if strongly persuaded of the truth of the position he supported. "He came to my lawyer's office," Molineux testified. Then Osborne made the classic cross-examiner's error, venturing a question calling for an answer that he could neither predict nor challenge: "Well, what did he say?" The defendant, glad of the opportunity, gave a devastating response: "He said that if he came to the conclusion that I had written the compromising paper, he would at once inform the district attorney and deliver me up."

All in all, the cross-examination was an unqualified triumph for the defendant. His father, the general, observed after his son left the stand: "Roland bore himself under fire like a true Molineux."

The old soldier's confidence was amply justified, for the jury acquitted Roland after twelve minutes' deliberation.

After his acquittal, Molineux gave up the paint business for literature, writing plays, stories, and poetry. In 1903 he published *The Room with the Little Door*, a collection of sketches based on his experiences in the Tombs prison and the death house at Sing Sing. Strange to say, it is a distinctly sunny work and even has good words to say in behalf of the "third degree", which he assured his readers was never applied to him. Critics hailed the book as the first fruit of a sensitive and promising young talent. David Belasco in 1913 produced Molineux's melodrama of prison life, *The Man Inside*.

A year later, the newspapers reported that Molineux had

escaped from a sanitorium in Babylon, Long Island, where he had been under treatment for a nervous breakdown and "had started for a run in the village, without trousers and dressed in running shirt and a bathrobe". With the consent of his father, he was committed to the King's Park State Hospital for the Insane, where he died in 1917. The hospital records attributed his death to general paralysis, cerebral type, due to syphilitic infection (general paresis).

If it is pardonable in retrospect to conclude that Roland Molineux's first jury was the wiser one, he can be seen as a murderer whose career anticipated by almost a century some of the most extraordinary phenomena of present-day American crime. In the details of his technique — the lacing of a painkiller with cyanide, the use of an ostensibly original sealed drug package, and the indirect means of delivery of the poison, he is the ancestor of the still-unknown murderer who killed seven people in the Chicago area in 1982 with poisoned capsules of the aspirin substitute, Extra-Strength Tylenol. Moreover, as a murder convict who was able to turn the experiences of imprisonment into a literary career, he blazed the trail for Jack Henry Abbott. In 1981 Abbott (who had stabbed a fellow inmate to death in 1967) was paroled in large part due to Norman Mailer's trumpeting of the literary merit of a collection of the convict's prison correspondence (published as *In the Belly of the Beast*). In both these cases, Molineux's modern successors have outdone him in horrors. The Tylenol murderer claimed many more victims and, so far as is known, had no grievances against any of them; and while Molineux's brief literary celebrity left no ill-effects except a few bad books, Abbott, only a few months after his release, killed again, stabbing an actor and part-time waiter in a dispute at a restaurant in lower Manhattan.

The Case of Oscar Slater

(Published in 1912)

Arthur Conan Doyle

IT IS IMPOSSIBLE to read and weigh the facts in connection with the conviction of Oscar Slater in May 1909, at the High Court in Edinburgh, without feeling deeply dissatisfied with the proceedings, and morally certain that justice was not done. Under the circumstances of Scotch law I am not clear how far any remedy exists, but it will, in my opinion, be a serious scandal if the man be allowed upon such evidence to spend his life in a convict prison. The verdict which led to his condemnation to death was given by a jury of fifteen, who voted: Nine for "Guilty", five for "Non-proven" and one for "Not Guilty". Under English law, this division of opinion would naturally have given cause for a new trial. In Scotland the man was condemned to death, he was only reprieved two days before his execution, and he is now working out a life sentence in Peterhead convict establishment. How far the verdict was a just one, the reader may judge for himself when he has perused a connected story of the case.

There lived in Glasgow in the year 1908, an old maiden lady named Miss Marion Gilchrist. She had lived for thirty years in the one flat, which was on the first floor in 15 Queen's Terrace. The flat above hers was vacant, and the only immediate neighbours were a family named Adams, living on the ground floor below, their house having a separate door which was close alongside the flat entrance. The old lady had one servant, named Helen Lambie, who was a girl twenty-one years of age. This girl had been with Miss Gilchrist for three or four years. By all accounts Miss Gilchrist was a most estimable person, leading a quiet and uneventful life. She was comfortably off, and she had one singular characteristic for a lady of her age

14 and 15 Queen's Terrace, Glasgow

The close door of Miss Gilchrist's house is on the left, the main door of Mr
Adam's house is on the right; the windows of the dining room are the
leftmost two above the close door.
(From the photograph produced in Court)

and surroundings, in that she had made a collection of
jewellery of considerable value. These jewels, which took the
form of brooches, rings, pendants, etc., were bought at
different times, extending over a considerable number of
years, from a reputable jeweller. I lay stress upon the fact, as
some wild rumour was circulated at the time that the old lady
might herself be a criminal receiver. Such an idea could not be
entertained. She seldom wore her jewellery save in single
pieces, and as her life was a retired one, it is difficult to see how
anyone outside a very small circle could have known of her
hoard. The value of this treasure was about three thousand
pounds. It was a fearful joy which she snatched from its
possession, for she more than once expressed apprehension
that she might be attacked and robbed. Her fears had the

Miss Marion Gilchrist
(*From the photograph produced in Court*)

practical result that she attached two patent locks to her front door, and that she arranged with the Adams family underneath that in case of alarm she would signal to them by knocking upon the floor.

It was the household practice that Lambie, the maid, should go out and get an evening paper for her mistress about seven o'clock each day. After bringing the paper she then usually went out again upon the necessary shopping. This routine was followed upon the night of 21 December. She left her mistress seated by the fire in the dining-room reading a magazine. Lambie took the keys with her, shut the flat door, closed the hall door downstairs, and was gone about ten minutes upon her errand. It is the events of those ten minutes which form the tragedy and the mystery which were so soon to engage the attention of the public.

According to the girl's evidence, it was a minute or two before seven when she went out. At about seven, Mr Arthur Adams and his two sisters were in their dining-room immediately below the room in which the old lady had been left. Suddenly they heard "a noise from above, then a very heavy fall, and then three sharp knocks". They were alarmed at the sound, and the young man at once set off to see if all was right. He ran out of his hall door, through the hall door of the flats, which was open, and so up to the first floor, where he found Miss Gilchrist's door shut. He rang three times without an answer. From within, however, he heard a sound which he compared to the breaking of sticks. He imagined therefore that the servant girl was within, and that she was engaged in her household duties. After waiting for a minute or two, he seems to have convinced himself that all was right. He therefore descended again and returned to his sisters, who persuaded him to go up once more to the flat. This he did and rang for the fourth time. As he was standing with his hand upon the bell, straining his ears and hearing nothing, someone approached up the stairs from below. It was the young servant-maid, Helen Lambie, returning from her errand. The two held council for a moment. Young Adams described the noise which had been heard. Lambie said that the pulleys of the clothes-lines in the kitchen must have given way. It was a singular explanation, since the kitchen was not above the dining-room of the Adams, and one would not expect any great noise from the fall of a cord which suspended sheets or towels. However, it was a moment of agitation, and the girl may have said the first explanation which came into her head. She then put her keys into the two safety locks and opened the door.

At this point there is a curious little discrepancy of evidence. Lambie is prepared to swear that she remained upon the mat beside young Adams. Adams is equally positive that she walked several paces down the hall. This inside hall was lit by a

The Dining Room. The cushion on the floor in the front of the fireplace
shows the position of the body
(*From the photograph produced in Court*)

gas, which, turned half up, and shining through a coloured
shade, gave a sufficient, but not a brilliant light. Says Adams:
"I stood at the door on the threshold, half in and half out, and
just when the girl had got past the clock to go into the kitchen,
a well-dressed man appeared. I did not suspect him, and she
said nothing; and he came up to me quite pleasantly. I did not
suspect anything wrong for the minute. I thought the man was
going to speak to me, till he got past me, and then I suspected
something wrong, and by that time the girl ran into the kitchen
and put the gas up and said it was all right, meaning her
pulleys. I said: 'Where is your mistress?' and she went into the
dining-room. She said: 'Oh! Come here!' I just went in and saw
this horrible spectacle."

The spectacle in question was the poor old lady lying upon
the floor close by the chair in which the servant had last seen
her. Her feet were towards the door, her head towards the

fireplace. She lay upon a hearth-rug, but a skin rug had been thrown across her head. Her injuries were frightful, nearly every bone of her face and skull being smashed. In spite of her dreadful wounds she lingered for a few minutes, but died without showing any sign of consciousness.

The murderer when he had first appeared had emerged from one of the two bedrooms at the back of the hall, the larger, or spare bedroom, not the old lady's room. On passing Adams upon the doormat, which he had done with the utmost coolness, he had at once rushed down the stair. It was a dark and drizzly evening, and it seems that he made his way along one or two quiet streets until he was lost in the more crowded thoroughfares. He had left no weapon nor possession of any sort in the old lady's flat, save a box of matches with which he had lit the gas in the bedroom from which he had come. In this bedroom a number of articles of value, including a watch, lay upon the dressing-table, but none of them had been touched. A box containing papers had been forced open, and these papers were found scattered upon the floor. If he were really in search of the jewels, he was badly informed, for these were kept among the dresses in the old lady's wardrobe. Later, a single crescent diamond brooch, an article worth perhaps forty or fifty pounds, was found to be missing. Nothing else was taken from the flat. It is remarkable that though the furniture round where the body lay was spattered with blood, and one would have imagined that the murderer's hands must have been stained, no mark was seen upon the half-consumed match with which he had lit the gas, nor upon the match box, the box containing papers, nor any other thing which he may have touched in the bedroom.

We come now to the all-important question of the description of the man seen at such close quarters by Adams and Lambie. Adams was short-sighted and had not his spectacles with him. His evidence at the trial ran thus:

"He was a man a little taller and a little broader than I am, not a well-built man but well-featured and clean-shaven, and I cannot exactly swear to his moustache, but if he had any it was very little. He was rather a commercial-traveller type, or perhaps a clerk, and I did not know but what he might be one of her friends. He had on dark trousers and a light overcoat. I could not say if it were fawn or grey. I do not recollect what sort of hat he had. He seemed gentlemanly and well-dressed. He had nothing in his hand so far as I could tell. I did not notice anything about his way of walking."

Helen Lambie, the other spectator, could give no information about the face (which rather bears out Adams's view as to her position), and could only say that he wore a round cloth hat, a three-quarter-length overcoat of a grey colour, and that he had some peculiarity in his walk. As the distance traversed by the murderer within sight of Lambie could be crossed in four steps, and as these steps were taken under circumstances of peculiar agitation, it is difficult to think that any importance could be attached to this last item in the description.

It is impossible to avoid some comment upon the actions of Helen Lambie during the incidents just narrated, which can only be explained by supposing that from the time she saw Adams waiting outside her door, her whole reasoning faculty had deserted her. First, she explained the great noise heard below: "The ceiling was like to crack," said Adams, by the fall of a clothes-line and its pulleys of attachment, which could not possibly, one would imagine, have produced any such effect. She then declares that she remained upon the mat, while Adams is convinced that she went right down the hall. On the appearance of the stranger she did not gasp out: "Who are you?" or any other sign of amazement, but allowed Adams to suppose by her silence that the man might be someone who had a right to be there. Finally, instead of rushing at once to see if her mistress was safe, she went into the kitchen, still apparently under the obsession of the pulleys. She informed Adams that they were all right, as if it mattered to any human being; thence she went into the spare bedroom, where she must have seen that robbery had been committed, since an open box lay in the middle of the floor. She gave no alarm, however, and it was only when Adams called out: "Where is your mistress?" that she finally went into the room of the murder. It must be admitted that this seems strange conduct, and only explicable, if it can be said to be explicable, by great want of intelligence and grasp of the situation.

On Tuesday, 22 December, the morning after the murder, the Glasgow police circulated a description of the murderer, founded upon the joint impressions of Adams and of Lambie. It ran thus:

> A man between 25 and 30 years of age, five foot eight or nine inches in height, slim build, dark hair, clean-shaven, dressed in light grey overcoat and dark cloth cap.

Four days later, however, upon Christmas Day, the police found themselves in a position to give a more detailed description:

> The man wanted is about 28 or 30 years of age, tall and thin, with his face shaved clear of all hair, while a distinctive feature is that his nose is slightly turned to one side. The witness thinks the twist is to the right side. He wore one of the popular tweed hats known as Donegal hats, and a fawn-coloured overcoat which might have been a waterproof, also dark trousers and brown boots.

The material from which these further points were gathered came from a young girl of fifteen, in humble life, named Mary Barrowman. According to this new evidence, the witness was passing the scene of the murder shortly after seven o'clock upon the fatal night. She saw a man run hurriedly down the steps, and he passed her under a lamp-post. The incandescent light shone clearly upon him. He ran on, knocking against the witness in his haste, and disappeared round a corner. On hearing later of the murder, she connected this incident with it. Her general recollections of the man were as given in the description, and the grey coat and cloth cap of the first two witnesses were given up in favour of the fawn coat and round Donegal hat of the young girl. Since she had seen no peculiarity in his walk, and they had seen none in his nose, there is really nothing the same in the two descriptions save the "clean-shaven", the "slim build" and the approximate age.

It was on the evening of Christmas Day that the police came at last upon a definite clue. It was brought to their notice that a German Jew of the assumed name of Oscar Slater had been endeavouring to dispose of the pawn ticket of a crescent diamond brooch of about the same value as the missing one. Also, that in a general way, he bore a resemblance to the published description. Still more hopeful did this clue appear when, upon raiding the lodgings in which this man and his mistress lived, it was found that they had left Glasgow that very night by the nine o'clock train, with tickets (over this point there was some clash of evidence) either for Liverpool or London. Three days later, the Glasgow police learned that the couple had actually sailed upon 26 December upon the *Lusitania* for New York under the name of Mr and Mrs Otto Sando. It must be admitted that in all these proceedings the Glasgow police showed considerable deliberation. The original information had been given at the Central Police Office shortly after six o'clock, and a detective was actually making enquiries at Slater's flat at seven-thirty, yet no watch was kept upon his movements, and he was allowed to leave between eight and nine, untraced and unquestioned. Even stranger was the Liverpool departure. He was known to have got away in the south-bound train upon the Friday evening. A great liner sails from Liverpool upon the Saturday. One would have imagined that early on the Saturday morning steps would have been taken to block his method of escape. However, as a fact, it was not done, and as it proved it is as well for the cause of justice, since it had the effect that two judicial processes were needed, an American and a Scottish, which enables an interesting comparison to be made between the evidence of the principal witnesses.

Oscar Slater was at once arrested upon arriving at New York, and his seven trunks of baggage were impounded and sealed. On the face of it there was a good case against him, for he had undoubtedly pawned a diamond brooch, and he had subsequently fled under a false name for America. The Glasgow police had reason to think that they had got their man. Two officers, accompanied by the witnesses to identity

Oscar Slater in 1908

— Adams, Lambie and Barrowman — set off at once to carry through the extradition proceedings and bring the suspect back to be tried for his offence. In the New York Court they first set eyes upon the prisoner, and each of them, in terms which will be afterwards described, expressed the opinion that he was at any rate exceedingly like the person they had seen in Glasgow. Their actual identification of him was vitiated by the fact that Adams and Barrowman had been shown his photographs before attending the Court, and also that he was led past them, an obvious prisoner, whilst they were waiting in the corridor. Still, however much one may discount the actual identification, it cannot be denied that each witness saw a close resemblance between the man before them and the man whom they had seen in Glasgow. So far at every stage the case against the accused was becoming more menacing. Any doubt as to extradition was speedily set at rest by the prisoner's announcement that he was prepared, without compulsion, to return to Scotland and to stand his trial. One may well refuse to give him any excessive credit for this surrender, since he may have been persuaded that things were going against him, but still the fact remains (and it was never, so far as I can trace, mentioned at his subsequent trial), that he gave himself up of his own free will to justice. On 21 February Oscar Slater was back in Glasgow once more, and on 3 May his trial took place at the High Court in Edinburgh.

But already the very bottom of the case had dropped out. The starting link of what had seemed an imposing chain had suddenly broken. It will be remembered that the original suspicion of Slater was founded upon the fact that he had pawned a crescent diamond brooch. The ticket was found upon him, and the brooch recovered. It was not the one which was missing from the room of the murdered woman, and it had belonged for years to Slater, who had repeatedly pawned it before. This was shown beyond all cavil or dispute. The case of the police might well seem desperate after this, since if Slater were indeed guilty, it would mean that by pure chance they had pursued the right man. The coincidence involved in such a supposition would seem to pass the limits of all probability.

Apart from this crushing fact, several of the other points of the prosecution had already shown themselves to be worthless. It had seemed at first that Slater's departure had been sudden and unpremeditated — the flight of a guilty man. It was quickly proved that this was not so. In the Bohemian clubs which he frequented — he was by profession a peddling jeweller and a man of disreputable, though not criminal habits — it had for weeks before the date of the crime been known that he purported to go to some business associates in America. A correspondence, which was produced, showed the arrangements which had been made, long before the crime, for his emigration, though it should be added that the actual determination of the date and taking of the ticket were subsequent to the tragedy.

This hurrying-up of the departure certainly deserves close scrutiny. According to the evidence of his mistress and of the servant, Slater had received two letters upon the morning of 21 December. Neither of these was produced at the trial. One was said to be from a Mr Rogers, a friend of Slater's in London, telling him that Slater's wife was bothering him for money. The second was said to be from one Devoto, a former partner of Slater's, asking him to join him in San Francisco. Even if the letters had been destroyed, one would imagine that these statements as to the letters could be disproved or corroborated by either the Crown or the defence. They are of considerable importance, as giving the alleged reasons why Slater hurried up a departure which had been previously announced as for January. I cannot find, however, that in the actual trial anything definite was ascertained upon the matter.

Another point had already been scored against the prosecution in that the seven trunks which contained the whole effects of the prisoner, yielded nothing of real importance. There were a felt hat and two cloth ones, but none which corresponded with the Donegal of the original description. A light-coloured waterproof coat was among the outfit. If the weapon with which the deed was done was carried off in the pocket of the assassin's overcoat — and it is difficult to say how else he could have carried it — then the pocket must, one would suppose, be crusted with blood, since the crime was a most sanguinary one. No such marks were discovered, nor were the police fortunate as to the weapon. It is true that a hammer was found in the trunk, but it was clearly shown to have been purchased in one of those cheap half-crown sets of tools which are tied upon a card, was an extremely light and fragile instrument, and utterly incapable in the eyes of commonsense of inflicting those terrific injuries which had shattered the old lady's skull. It was said by the prosecution to bear some marks of having been scraped or cleaned, but this was vigorously denied by the defence, and the police do not appear to have pushed the matter to the obvious test of removing the metal work, when they must, had this been indeed the weapon, have certainly found some soakage of blood into the wood under the edges of the iron cheeks or head. But a glance at a facsimile of this puny weapon would

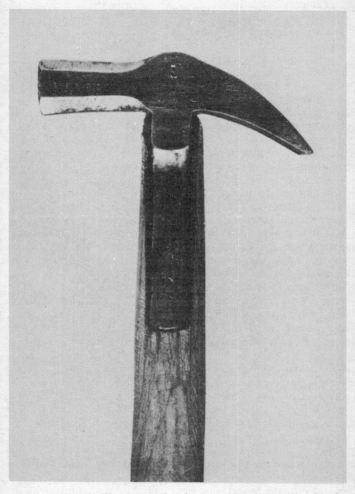

Head of hammer produced in Court (actual size)

convince an impartial person that any task beyond fixing a tin-tack, or cracking a small bit of coal, would be above its strength. It may fairly be said that before the trial had begun, the three important points of the pawned jewel, the supposed flight, and the evidence from clothing and weapon, had each either broken down completely, or become exceedingly attenuated.

Let us see now what there was upon the other side. The evidence for the prosecution really resolved itself into two sets of witnesses for identification. The first set were those who had actually seen the murderer, and included Adams, Helen Lambie, and the girl Barrowman. The second set consisted of twelve people who had, at various dates, seen a man frequenting the street in which Miss Gilchrist lived, and loitering in a suspicious manner before the house. All of these, some with confidence, but most of them with reserve, were prepared to identify the prisoner with this unknown man. What the police never could produce, however, was the essential thing, and that was the least connecting link between Slater and Miss Gilchrist, or any explanation how a foreigner in Glasgow could even know of the existence, to say nothing of the wealth, of a retired old lady, who had few acquaintances and seldom left her guarded flat.

It is notorious that nothing is more tricky than evidence of identification. In the [Adolf] Beck case there were, if I remember right, some ten witnesses who had seen the real criminal under normal circumstances, and yet they were all prepared to swear to the wrong man. In the case of Oscar Slater, the first three witnesses saw their man under conditions of excitement, while the second group saw the loiterer in the street under various lights, and in a fashion which was always more or less casual. It is right, therefore, that in assigning its due weight to this evidence, one should examine it with some care. We shall first take the three people who actually saw the murderer.

There seems to have been some discrepancy between them from the first, since, as has already been pointed out, the description published from the data of Adams and Lambie, was modified after Barrowman had given her information. Adams and Lambie said:

> A man between twenty-five and thirty years of age, 5 feet 8 or 9 inches in height, slim build, dark hair, clean-shaven, dressed in light grey overcoat and dark cloth cap.

After collaboration with Barrowman the description became:

> Twenty-eight or thirty years of age, tall and thin, clean-shaven, his nose slightly turned to one side. Wore one of the popular round tweed hats known as Donegal hats, and a fawn-coloured overcoat which might have been a waterproof, also dark trousers and brown boots.

Apart from the additions in the second description there are, it will be observed, two actual discrepancies in the shape of the hat and the colour of the coat.

As to how far either of these descriptions tallies with Slater, it may be stated here that the accused was thirty-seven years of age, that he was above the medium height, that his nose was not twisted, but was depressed at the end, as if it had at some time been broken, and finally that eight witnesses were called upon to prove that, on the date of the murder, the accused wore a short but noticeable moustache.

I have before me a verbatim stenographic report of the proceedings in New York and also in Edinburgh, furnished by the kindness of Shaughnessy & Co., solicitors, of Glasgow, who are still contending for the interests of their unfortunate client. I will here compare the terms of the identification in the two Courts.

Helen Lambie, New York, 26 January 1909:

Q. Do you see the man here you saw there?
A. One is very suspicious, if anything.
Q. Describe him.
A. The clothes he had on that night he hasn't got on today — but his face I could not tell. I never saw his face.

Having described a peculiarity of walk, she was asked:

Q. Is that man in the room?
A. Yes, he is, sir.
Q. Point him out.
A. I would not like to say —
(After some pressure and argument, she pointed to Slater, who had been led past her in the corridor between two officers, when both she and Barrowman had exclaimed: "That is the man," or "I could nearly swear that is the man.")
Q. Didn't you say you did not see the man's face?
A. Neither I did. I saw the walk.

The reader must bear in mind that Lambie's only chance of seeing the man's walk was in the four steps or so down the passage. It was never at any time shown that there was any marked peculiarity about Slater's walk.

Now take Helen Lambie's identification in Edinburgh, 9 May 1909:

Q. How did you identify him in America?
A. By his walk and height, his dark hair and the side of his face.
Q. You were not quite sure of him at first in America?
A. Yes, I was quite sure.
Q. Why did you say you were only suspicious?
A. It was a mistake.
Q. What did you mean in America by saying that you never saw his face if, in point of fact, you did see it so as to help you to recognize it? What did you mean?
A. Nothing.

On further cross-examination she declared that when she said that she had never seen the man's face she meant that she had never seen the "broad of it" but had seen it sideways.

Here it will be observed that Helen Lambie's evidence had greatly stiffened during the three months between the New York and the Edinburgh proceedings. In so aggressively positive a frame of mind was she on the later occasion, that, on being shown Slater's overcoat and asked if it resembled the murderer's, she answered twice over: "That is the coat," although it had not yet been unrolled, and though it was not light grey, which was the colour in her own original description. It should not be forgotten in dealing with the evidence of Lambie and Adams that they are utterly disagreed as to so easily fixed a thing as their own proceedings after the hall door was opened, Adams swearing that Lambie walked to nearly the end of the hall, and Lambie that she remained upon the doormat. Without deciding which was right, it is clear that the incident must shake one's confidence on one or other of them as a witness.

In the case of Adams the evidence was given with moderation, and was substantially the same in America and in Scotland.

"I couldn't say positively. This man [indicating Slater] is not at all unlike him."
Q. Did you notice a crooked nose?
A. No.
Q. Anything remarkable about his walk?
A. No.
Q. You don't swear this is the man you saw?
A. No, sir. He resembles the man, that is all that I can say.

In reply to the same general questions in Edinburgh, he said:

"I would not like to swear he is the man. I am a little near-sighted. He resembles the man closely."

Barrowman, the girl of fifteen, had met the man presumed to be the murderer in the street, and taken one passing glance at him under a gas lamp on a wet December's night — difficult circumstances for an identification. She used these words in New York:

"That man here is something like him," which she afterwards amended to "very like him". She admitted that a picture of the man she was expected to identify had been shown to her before she came into the Court. Her one point by which she claimed to recognize the man was the crooked nose.

This crooked nose was not much more apparent to others than the peculiarity of walk which so greatly impressed Helen Lambie that, after seeing half a dozen steps of it, she could identify it with confidence. In Edinburgh Barrowman, like Lambie, was very much more certain than in New York. The further they got from the event, the easier apparently did recognition become. "Yes, that is the man who knocked against me that night," she said. It is remarkable that both these females, Lambie and Barrowman, swore that though they were thrown together in this journey out to New York, and actually shared the same cabin, they never once talked of the object of their mission or compared notes as to the man they were about to identify. For girls of the respective ages of fifteen and twenty-one, this certainly furnishes a unique example of self-restraint.

These, then, are the three identifications by the only people who saw the murderer. Had the diamond brooch clue been authentic, and these identifications come upon the top of it, they would undoubtedly have been strongly corroborative. But when the brooch has been shown to be a complete mistake, I really do not understand how anyone could accept such half-hearted recognitions as being enough to establish the identity and guilt of the prisoner.

There remains the so-called identification by twelve witnesses who had seen a man loitering in the street during the weeks before the crime had been committed. I have said a "so-called" identification, for the proceedings were farcical as a real test of recognition. The witnesses had seen portraits of the accused. They were well aware that he was a foreigner, and then they were asked to pick out his swarthy Jewish physiognomy from among nine Glasgow policemen and two railway officials. Naturally they did it without hesitation, since this man was more like the dark individual whom they had seen and described than the others could be.

Read their own descriptions, however, of the man they had seen, with the details of his clothing, and they will be found in many respects to differ from each other on one hand, and in many from Slater on the other. Here is a synopsis of their impressions:

Mrs McHaffie — Dark. Moustached, light overcoat, not waterproof, check trousers, spats. Black bowler hat. Nose normal.

Miss M. McHaffie — Seen at same time and same description. Was only prepared at first to say there was some resemblance, but "had been thinking it over, and concluded that he was the man".

Miss A.M. McHaffie — Same as before. Had heard the man speak and noticed nothing in his accent. (Prisoner has a strong German accent.)

Madge McHaffie (belongs to the same family) — Dark, moustached, nose normal. Check trousers, fawn overcoat and spats. Black bowler hat. "The prisoner was fairly like the man."

In connection with the identification of these four witnesses it is to be observed that neither check trousers nor spats were found in the prisoner's luggage. As the murderer was described as being dressed in dark trousers, there was no possible reason why these clothes, if Slater owned them, should have been destroyed.

Constable Brien — Claimed to know the prisoner by sight. Says he was the man he saw loitering. Light coat and a hat. It was a week before the crime, and he was loitering eighty yards from the scene of it. He picked him out among five constables as the man he had seen.

Constable Walker — Had seen the loiterer across the street, never nearer, and after dark in December. Thought at first he was someone else whom he knew. Had heard that the man he had to identify was of foreign appearance. Picked him out from a number of detectives. The man seen had a moustache.

Euphemia Cunningham — Very dark, sallow, heavy featured. Clean-shaven. Nose normal. Dark tweed coat. Green cap with peak.

W. Campbell — Had been with the previous witness. Corroborated. "There was a general resemblance between the prisoner and the man, but he could not positively identify him."

Alex Gillies — Sallow, dark-haired and clean-shaven. Fawn

coat. Cap. "The prisoner resembled him, but witness could not say he was the same man."

R.B. Bryson — Black coat and vest. Black bowler hat. No overcoat. Black moustache with droop. Sallow, foreign. (This witness had seen the man the night before the murder. He appeared to be looking up at Miss Gilchrist's windows.)

A. Nairn — Broad shoulders, long neck. Dark hair. Motor cap. Light overcoat to knees. Never saw the man's face. "Oh! I will not swear in fact, but I am certain he is the man I saw — but I will not swear."

Mrs Liddell — Peculiar nose. Clear complexion, not sallow. Dark, clean-shaven, brown tweed cap. Brown tweed coat with hemmed edge. Delicate man "rather drawn together". She believed that prisoner was the man. Saw him in the street immediately before the murder.

These are the twelve witnesses as to the identify of the mysterious stranger. In the first place there is no evidence whatever that this lounger in the street had really anything to do with the murder. It is just as probable that he had some vulgar amour, and was waiting for his girl to run out to him. What could a man who was planning murder hope to gain by standing nights beforehand eighty and a hundred yards away from the place in the darkness? But supposing that we waive this point and examine the plain question as to whether Slater was the same man as the loiterer, we find ourselves faced by a mass of difficulties and contradictions. Two of the most precise witnesses were Nairn and Bryson, who saw the stranger upon the Sunday night preceding the murder. Upon that night Slater had an unshaken alibi, vouched for not only by the girl, Antoine, with whom he lived, and their servant, Schmalz, but by an acquaintance, Samuel Reid, who had been with him from six to ten-thirty. This positive evidence, which was quite unshaken in cross-examination, must completely destroy the surmises of the stranger and Slater. Then come the four witnesses of the McHaffie family who are all strong upon check trousers and spats, articles of dress which were never traced to the prisoner. Finally, apart from the discrepancies about the moustache, there is a mixture of bowler hats, green caps, brown caps, and motor caps which leave a most confused and indefinite impression in the mind. Evidence of this kind might be of some value if supplementary to some strong ascertained fact, but to attempt to build upon such an identification alone is to construct the whole case upon shifting sand.

The reader has already a grasp of the facts, but some fresh details came out at the trial which may be enumerated here. They have to be lightly touched upon within the limits of such an argument as this, but those who desire a fuller summary will find it in an account of the trial published by Hodge of Edinburgh, and ably edited by William Roughead, W.S. On this book and on the verbatim precognitions and shorthand account of the American proceedings, I base my own examination of the case. First, as to Slater's movements upon the day of the crime. He began the day, according to the account of himself and the women, by the receipt of the two letters already referred to, which caused him to hasten his journey to America. The whole day seems to have been occupied by preparations for his impending departure. He gave his servant Schmalz notice as from next Saturday. Before five (as was shown by the postmark upon the envelope), he wrote to a post office in London, where he had some money on deposit. At 6.12 a telegram was sent in his name and presumably by him from the Central Station to Dent, London, for his watch, which was being repaired. According to the evidence of two witnesses, he was seen in a billiard room at 6.20. The murder, it will be remembered, was done at seven. He remained about ten minutes in the billiard room, and left some time between 6.30 and 6.40. Rathman, one of these witnesses, deposed that he had at the time a moustache about a quarter of an inch long, which was so noticeable that no one could take him for a clean-shaven man. Antoine, his mistress, and Schmalz, the servant, both deposed that Slater dined at home at seven o'clock. The evidence of the girl is no doubt suspect, but there was no possible reason why the dismissed servant Schmalz should perjure herself for the sake of her ex-employer. The distance between Slater's flat and that of

Miss Gilchrist is about a quarter of a mile. From the billiard room to Slater's flat is about a mile. He had to go for the hammer and bring it back, unless he had it jutting out of his pocket all day. But unless the evidence of the two women is entirely set aside, enough has been said to show that there was no time for the commission by him of such a crime and the hiding of the traces which it would leave behind it. At 9.45 that night, Slater was engaged in his usual occupation of trying to raise the wind at some small gambling club. The club-master saw no discomposure about his dress (which was the same as, according to the Crown, he had done this bloody crime in), and swore that he was then wearing a short moustache "like stubble", thus corroborating Rathman. It will be remembered that Lambie and Barrowman both swore that the murderer was clean-shaven.

On 24 December, three days after the murder, Slater was shown at Cook's Office, bargaining for a berth in the *Lusitania* for his so-called wife and himself. He made no secret that he was going by that ship, but gave his real name and address and declared finally that he would take his berth in Liverpool, which he did. Among other confidants as to the ship was a barber, the last person one would think to whom secrets would be confided. Certainly, if this were a flight, it is hard to say what an open departure would be. In Liverpool he took his passage under the assumed name of Otto Sando. This he did, according to his own account, because he had reason to fear pursuit from his real wife, and wished to cover his traces. This may or may not be the truth, but it is undoubtedly the fact that Slater, who was a disreputable, rolling-stone of a man, had already assumed several aliases in the course of his career. It is to be noted that there was nothing at all secret about his departure from Glasgow, and that he carried off all his luggage with him in a perfectly open manner.

The reader is now in possession of the main facts, save those which are either unessential or redundant. It will be observed that save for the identifications, the value of which can be estimated, there is really no single point of connection between the crime and the alleged criminal. It may be argued that the existence of the hammer is such a point; but what household in the land is devoid of a hammer? It is to be remembered that if Slater committed the murder with this hammer, he must have taken it with him in order to commit the crime, since it could be no use to him in forcing an entrance. But what man in his senses, planning a deliberate murder, would take with him a weapon which was light, frail, and so long that it must project from any pocket? The nearest lump of stone upon the road would serve his purpose better than that. Again, it must in its blood-soaked condition have been in his pocket when he came away from the crime. The Crown never attempted to prove either blood-stains in a pocket, or the fact that any clothes had been burned. If Slater destroyed clothes, he would naturally have destroyed the hammer, too. Even one of the two medical witnesses of the prosecution was driven to say that he should not have expected such a weapon to cause such wounds.

It may well be that in this summary of the evidence, I may seem to have stated the case entirely from the point of view of the defence. In reply, I would only ask the reader to take the trouble to read the extended evidence. (*Trial of Oscar Slater*, Hodge & Co., Edinburgh.) If he will do so, he will realize that without a conscious mental effort towards special pleading, there is no other way in which the story can be told. The facts are on one side. The conjectures, the unsatisfactory identifications, the damaging flaws, and the very strong prejudices upon the other.

Now for the trial itself. The case was opened for the Crown by the Lord-Advocate, in a speech which faithfully represented the excited feeling of the time. It was vigorous to the point of being passionate, and its effect upon the jury was reflected in their ultimate verdict. The Lord-Advocate spoke, as I understand, without notes, a procedure which may well add to eloquence while subtracting from accuracy. It is to this fact that one must attribute a most fatal misstatement which could not fail, coming under such circumstances from so high an authority, to make a deep impression upon his hearers. For some reason, this misstatement does not appear to have been corrected at the moment by either the judge or the defending counsel. It was the one really damaging allegation — so damaging that had I myself been upon the jury and believed it to be true, I should have recorded my verdict against the prisoner, and yet this one fatal point had no substance at all in fact. In this incident alone, there seems to me to lie good ground for a revision of the sentence, or a reference of the facts to some Court or Committee of Appeal. Here is the extract from the Lord-Advocate's speech to which I allude:

At this time he had given his name to Cook's people in Glasgow as Oscar Slater. On 25 December, the day he was to go back to Cook's Office, his name and his description and all the rest of it appear in the Glasgow papers, and he sees that the last thing in the world that he ought to do, if he studies his own safety, is to go back to Cook's Office as Oscar Slater. He accordingly proceeds to pack up all his goods and effects upon the 25th. So far as we know, he never leaves the house from the time he sees the paper until a little after six o'clock, when he goes down to the Central Station.

Here the allegation is clearly made and it is repeated later that Oscar Slater's name was in the paper, and that, subsequently to that, he fled. Such a flight would clearly be an admission of guilt. The point is of enormous, even vital, importance. And yet on examination of the dates, it will be found that there is absolutely no foundation for it. It was not until the evening of the 25th that even the police heard of the existence of Slater, and it was nearly a week later that his name appeared in the papers, he being already far out upon the Atlantic. What did appear upon the 25th was the description of the murderer, already quoted: "with his face shaved clean of all hair", etc., Slater at that time having a marked moustache. Why should he take such a description to himself, or why should he forbear to carry out a journey which he had already prepared for? The point goes for absolutely nothing when examined, and yet if the minds of the jury were at all befogged as to the dates, the definite assertion of the Lord-Advocate, twice repeated, that Slater's name had been published before his flight, was bound to have a most grave and prejudiced effect.

91

Some of the Lord-Advocate's other statements are certainly surprising. Thus he says: "The prisoner is hopelessly unable to produce a single witness who says that he was anywhere else than at the scene of the murder that night." Let us test this assertion. Here is the evidence of Schmalz, the servant, verbatim. I may repeat that this woman was under no known obligations to Slater and had just received notice from him. The evidence of the mistress that Slater dined in the flat at seven on the night of the murder I pass, but I do not understand why Schmalz's positive corroboration should be treated by the Lord-Advocate as non-existent. The prisoner might well be "hopeless" if his witnesses were to be treated so. Could anything be more positive than this?

Q. Did he usually come home to dinner?
A. Yes, always. Seven o'clock was the usual hour.
Q. Was it sometimes nearly eight?
A. It was my fault. Mr Slater was in.
Q. But owing to your fault, was it about eight before it was served?
A. No. Mr Slater was in after seven, and was waiting for dinner.

This seems very definite. The murder was committed about seven. The murderer may have regained the street about ten minutes or quarter past seven. It was some distance to Slater's flat. If he had done the murder he could hardly have reached it before half-past seven at the earliest. Yet Schmalz says he was in at seven, and so does Antoine. The evidence of the woman may be good or bad, but it is difficult to understand how anyone could state that the prisoner was "hopelessly unable to produce, etc." What evidence could he give, save that of everyone who lived with him?

For the rest, the Lord-Advocate had an easy task in showing that Slater was a worthless fellow, that he lived with and possibly on a woman of easy virtue, that he had several times changed his name, and that generally he was an unsatisfactory Bohemian. No actual criminal record was shown against him. Early in his speech, the Lord-Advocate remarked that he would show later how Slater may have come to know that Miss Gilchrist owned the jewels. No further reference appears to have been made to the matter, and his promise was therefore never fulfilled, though it is clearly of the utmost importance. Later, he stated that from the appearance of the wounds, they must have been done by a small hammer. There is no "must" in the matter, for it is clear that many other weapons, a burglar's jemmy, for example, would have produced the same effect. He then makes the good point that the prisoner dealt in precious stones, and could therefore dispose of the proceeds of such a robbery. The criminal, he added, was clearly someone who had no acquaintance with the inside of the house, and did not know where the jewels were kept. "That answers to the prisoner." It also, of course, answers to practically every man in Scotland. The Lord-Advocate then gave a summary of the evidence as to the man seen by various witnesses in the street. "Gentlemen, *if that was the prisoner*, how do you account for his presence there?" Of course, the whole point lies in the italicized phrase. There was, it must be admitted, a consensus of opinion among the witnesses that the prisoner was the man. But what was it compared with the consensus of opinion which wrongfully condemned Beck to penal servitude? The counsel laid considerable stress upon the fact that Mrs Liddell (one of the Adams family) had seen a man only a few minutes before the murder, loitering in the street, and identified him as Slater. The dress of the man seen in the street was very different from that given as the murderer's. He had a heavy tweed-mixture coat of a brownish hue, and a brown peaked cap. The original identification by Mrs Liddell was conveyed in the words: "One, slightly," when she was asked if any of a group at the police station resembled the man she had seen. Afterwards, like every other female witness, she became more positive. She declared that she had the clearest recollection of the man's face, and yet refused to commit herself as to whether he was shaven or moustached.

We have then the recognitions of Lambie, Adams and Barrowman, with their limitations and developments, which have been already discussed. Then comes the question of the so-called "flight" and the change of name upon the steamer. Had the prisoner been a man who had never before changed his name, this incident would be more striking. But the short glimpse we obtain of his previous life shows several changes of name, and it has not been suggested that each of them was the consequence of a crime. He seems to have been in debt in Glasgow and he also appears to have had reasons for getting away from the pursuit of an ill-used wife. The Lord-Advocate said that the change of name "could not be explained consistently with innocence". That may be true enough, but the change can surely be explained on some cause less grave than murder. Finally, after showing very truly that Slater was a great liar and that not a word he said need be believed unless there were corroboration, the Lord-Advocate wound up with the words: "My submission to you is that his guilt has been brought fairly home to him, that no shadow of doubt exists, that there is no reasonable doubt that he was the perpetrator of this foul murder." The verdict showed that the jury, under the spell of the Lord-Advocate's eloquence, shared this view, but, viewing it in colder blood, it is difficult to see upon what grounds he made so confident an assertion.

Mr M'Clure, who conducted the defence, spoke truly when, in opening his speech, he declared that "he had to fight a most unfair fight against public prejudice, roused with a fury I do not remember to have seen in any other case". Still he fought this fight bravely and with scrupulous moderation. His appeals were all to reason and never to emotion. He showed how clearly the prisoner had expressed his intention of going to America, weeks before the murder, and how every preparation had been made. On the day after the murder he had told witnesses that he was going to America and had discussed the advantages of various lines, finally telling one of them the particular boat in which he did eventually travel, curious proceedings for a fugitive from justice. Mr M'Clure described the movements of the prisoner on the night of the murder, after the crime had been committed, showing that he was wearing the very clothes in which the theory of the prosecution made him do the deed, as if such a deed could be done without leaving its traces. He showed, incidentally (it is a small point, but a human one), that one of the last actions of Slater in Glasgow was to take great trouble to get an English five-pound note in order to send it as a Christmas present to his parents in Germany. A man who could do this was not all bad. Finally, Mr M'Clure exposed very clearly the many discrepancies as to identification and warned the jury solemnly as to the dangers which have been so often proved to lurk in this class of evidence. Altogether, it was a broad, comprehensive reply, though where so many points were involved, it is natural that some few may have been overlooked. One does not, for example, find the counsel as insistent as one might expect upon such points as, the failure of the Crown to show how Slater could have known anything at all about the existence of Miss Gilchrist and her jewels, how he got into the flat, and what became of the brooch which, according to their theory, he had carried off. It is ungracious to suggest any additions to so earnest a defence, and no doubt one who is dependent upon printed accounts of the matter may miss points which were actually made, but not placed upon record.

Only on one point must Mr M'Clure's judgement be questioned, and that is on the most difficult one which a criminal counsel has ever to decide. He did not place his man in the box. This should very properly be taken as a sign of weakness. I have no means of saying what considerations led Mr M'Clure to this determination. It certainly told against his client. In the masterly memorial for reprieve drawn up by Slater's solicitor, the late Mr Spiers, it is stated with the full inner knowledge which that solicitor had, that Slater was all along anxious to give evidence on his own behalf. "He was advised by his counsel not to do so, but not from any knowledge of guilt. He had undergone the strain of a four days' trial. He speaks rather broken English, although quite intelligible — with a foreign accent, and he had been in custody since January." It must be admitted that these reasons are very unconvincing. It is much more probable that the counsel decided that the purely negative evidence which his client could give upon the crime would be dearly paid for by the long recital of sordid amours and blackguard experiences which would be drawn from him on cross-examination and have the most damning effect upon the minds of a respectable Edinburgh jury. And yet, perhaps, counsel did not sufficiently consider the prejudice which is excited — and rightly excited — against the prisoner who shuns the box. Some of this prejudice might have been removed if it had been made more clear that Slater had volunteered to come over and stand his trial of his own free will, without waiting for the verdict of the extradition proceedings.

There remains the summing up of Lord Guthrie. His Lordship threw out the surmise that the assassin may well have gone to the flat without any intention of murder. This is certainly possible, but in the highest degree improbable. He commented with great severity upon Slater's general character. In his summing-up of the case, he recapitulated the familiar facts in an impartial fashion, concluding with the words, "I suppose that you all think that the prisoner possibly is the murderer. You may very likely all think that he probably is the murderer. That, however, will not entitle you to convict him. The Crown have undertaken to prove that he is the murderer. That is the question you have to consider. If you think there is no reasonable doubt about it, you will convict him; if you think there is, you will acquit him."

In an hour and ten minutes the jury had made up their mind. By a majority they found the prisoner guilty. Out of fifteen, nine, as was afterwards shown, were for guilty, five for non-proven, and one for not guilty. By English law, a new trial would have been needed, ending, possibly, as in the [William] Gardiner case, in the complete acquittal of the prisoner. By Scotch law the majority verdict held good.

"I know nothing about the affair, absolutely nothing," cried the prisoner in a frenzy of despair. "I never heard the name. I know nothing about the affair. I do not know how I could be connected with the affair. I know nothing about it. I came from America on my own account. I can say no more."

Sentence of death was then passed.

The verdict was, it is said, a complete surprise to most of those in the Court, and certainly is surprising when examined after the event. I do not see how any reasonable man can carefully weigh the evidence and not admit that when the unfortunate prisoner cried, "I know nothing about it," he was possibly, and even probably, speaking the literal truth. Consider the monstrous coincidence which is involved in his guilt, the coincidence that the police, owing to their mistake over the brooch, by pure chance started out in pursuit of the right man. Which is *a priori* the more probable: That such an unheard-of million-to-one coincidence should have occurred, Or, that the police, having committed themselves to the theory that he was the murderer, refused to admit that they were wrong when the bottom fell out of the original case, and persevered in the hope that vague identifications of a queer-looking foreigner would justify their original action? Outside these identifications, I must repeat once again there is nothing to couple Slater with the murder, or to show that he ever knew, or could have known, that such a person as Miss Gilchrist existed.

The admirable memorial for a reprieve drawn up by the solicitors for the defence was signed by 20,000 members of the public, and had the effect of changing the death sentence to one of penal servitude for life. The sentence was passed on 6 May. For twenty days the man was left in doubt, and the written reprieve only arrived on 26 May, within twenty-four hours of the time for the execution. On July 8 Slater was conveyed to the Peterhead Convict prison. There he has now been for three years, and there he still remains.

I cannot help in my own mind comparing the case of Oscar Slater with another, which I had occasion to examine — that of George Edalji. I must admit that they are not of the same class. George Edalji was a youth of exemplary character. Oscar Slater was a blackguard. George Edalji was physically incapable of the crime for which he suffered three years' imprisonment (years for which he has not received, after his innocence was established, one shilling of compensation from the nation). Oscar Slater might conceivably have committed the murder, but the balance of proof and probability seems entirely against it. Thus, one cannot feel the same burning sense of injustice over the matter. And yet I trust for the sake of our character not only for justice, but for intelligence, that the judgment may in some way be reconsidered and the man's present punishment allowed to atone for those irregularities of life which helped to make his conviction possible.

Before leaving the case it is interesting to see how far this curious crime may be reconstructed and whether any possible light can be thrown upon it. Using second-hand material, one cannot hope to do more than indicate certain possibilities which may already have been considered and tested by the police. The trouble, however, with all police prosecutions is that, having once got what they imagine to be their man, they are not very open to any line of investigation which might lead to other conclusions. Everything which will not fit into the official theory is liable to be excluded. One might make a few isolated comments on the case which may at least give rise to some interesting trains of thought.

One question which has to be asked was whether the assassin was after the jewels at all. It might be urged that the type of man described by the spectators was by no means that of the ordinary thief. When he reached the bedroom and lit the gas, he did not at once seize the watch and rings which were lying openly exposed upon the dressing-table. He did not pick up a half-sovereign which was lying on the dining-room table. His attention was given to a wooden box, the lid of which he wrenched open. (This, I think, was "the breaking of sticks" heard by Adams.) The papers in it were strewed on the ground. Were the papers his object, and the final abstraction of one diamond brooch a mere blind? Personally, I can only point out the possibility of such a solution. On the other hand, it might be urged, if the thief's action seems inconsequential, that Adams had rung and that he already found himself in a desperate situation. It might be said also that, save a will, it would be difficult to imagine any paper which would account for such an enterprise, while the jewels, on the other hand, were an obvious mark for whoever knew of their existence.

Presuming that the assassin was indeed after the jewels, it is very instructive to note his knowledge of their location, and also its limitations. Why did he go straight into the spare bedroom where the jewels were actually kept? The same question may be asked with equal force if we consider that he was after the papers. Why the spare bedroom? Any knowledge gathered from outside (by a watcher in the back-yard, for example) would go to the length of ascertaining which was the old lady's room. One would expect a robber who had gained his information thus, to go straight to that chamber. But this man did not do so. He went straight to the unlikely room in which both jewels and papers actually were. Is not this remarkably suggestive? Does it not presuppose a previous acquaintance with the inside of the flat and the ways of its owner?

But now note the limitations of the knowledge. If it were the jewels he was after, he knew what room they were in, but not in what part of the room. A fuller knowledge would have told him they were kept in the wardrobe. And yet he searched a box. If he was after papers, his information was complete; but if he was indeed after the jewels, then we can say that he had the knowledge of one who is conversant, but not intimately conversant, with the household arrangements. To this we may add that he would seem to have shown ignorance of the habits of the inmates, or he would surely have chosen Lambie's afternoon or evening out for his attempt, and not have done it at a time when the girl was bound to be back within a very few minutes. What men had ever visited the house? The number must have been very limited. What friends? what tradesmen? what plumbers? Who brought back the jewels after they had been stored with the jewellers when the old lady went every year to the country? One is averse to throw out vague suspicions which may give pain to innocent people, and yet it is clear that there are lines of inquiry here which should be followed up, however negative the results.

How did the murderer get in if Lambie is correct in thinking that she shut the doors? I cannot get away from the conclusion that he had duplicate keys. In that case all becomes comprehensible, for the old lady — whose faculties were quite normal — would hear the lock go and would not be alarmed, thinking that Lambie had returned before her time. Thus, she would only know her danger when the murderer rushed into the room, and would hardly have time to rise, receive the first blow, and fall, as she was found, beside the chair, upon which she had been sitting. That is intelligible. But if he had not the keys, consider the difficulties. If the old lady had opened the flat door her body would have been found in the passage. Therefore, the police were driven to the hypothesis that the old lady heard the ring, opened the lower stair door from above (as can be done in all Scotch flats), opened the flat door, never looked over the lighted stair to see who was coming up, but returned to her chair and her magazine, leaving the door open, and a free entrance to the murderer. This is possible, but is it not in the highest degree improbable? Miss Gilchrist was nervous of robbery and would not neglect obvious precautions. The ring came immediately after the maid's departure. She could hardly have thought that it was her returning, the less so as the girl had the keys and would not need to ring. If she went as far as the hall door to open it, she only had to take another step to see who was ascending the stair. Would she not have taken it if it were only to say: "What, have you forgotten your keys?" That a nervous old lady should throw open both doors, never look to see who her visitor was, and return to her dining-room is very hard to believe.

And look at it from the murderer's point of view. He had planned out his proceedings. It is notorious that it is the easiest thing in the world to open the lower door of a Scotch flat. The blade of any penknife will do that. If he was to depend upon ringing to get at his victim, it was evidently better for him to ring at the upper door, as otherwise the chance would seem very great that she would look down, see him coming up the stair, and shut herself in. On the other hand, if he were at the upper door and she answered it, he had only to push his way in. Therefore, the latter would be his course if he rang at all. And yet the police theory is that though he rang, he rang from below. It is not what he would do, and if he did do it, it would be most unlikely that he would get in. How could he suppose that the old lady would do so incredible a thing as leave her door open and return to her reading? If she waited, she might even up to the last instant have shut the door in his face. If one weighs all these reasons, one can hardly fail, I think, to come to the conclusion that the murderer had keys, and that the old lady never rose from her chair until the last instant, because, hearing the keys in the door, she took it for granted that the maid had come back. But if he had keys, how did he get the mould, and how did he get them made? There is a line of inquiry here. The only conceivable alternatives are, that the murderer was actually concealed in the flat when Lambie came out, and of that there is no evidence whatever, or that the visitor was some one whom the old lady knew, in which case he would naturally have been admitted.

There are still one or two singular points which invite comment. One of these, which I have incidentally mentioned, is that neither the match, the match-box, nor the box opened in the bedroom showed any marks of blood. Yet the crime had been an extraordinarily bloody one. This is certainly very singular. An explanation given by Dr Adams, who was the first medical man to view the body, is worthy of attention. He considered that the wounds might have been inflicted by prods downwards from the leg of a chair, in which case the seat of the chair would preserve the clothes and to some extent the hands of the murderer from blood-stains. The condition of one of the chairs seemed to him to favour this supposition. The explanation is ingenious, but I must confess that I cannot understand how such wounds could be inflicted by such an instrument. There were in particular a number of spindle-shaped cuts with a bridge of skin between them which are very suggestive. My first choice as to the weapon which inflicted these would be a burglar's jemmy, which is bifurcated at one end, while the blow which pushed the poor woman's eye into her brain would represent a thrust from the other end. Failing a jemmy, I should choose a hammer, but a very different one from the toy thing from a half-crown card of tools which was exhibited in Court. Surely common sense would say that such an instrument could burst an eyeball, but could not possibly drive it deep into the brain, since the short head could not penetrate nearly so far. The hammer which I would reconstruct from the injuries would be what they call, I believe, a plasterer's hammer, short in the handle, long and strong in the head, with a broad fork behind. But how such a weapon could be used without the user bearing marks of it, is more than I can say. It has never been explained why a rug was laid over the murdered woman. The murderer, as his conduct before Lambie and Adams showed, was a perfectly cool person. It is at least possible that he used the rug as a shield between him and his victim while he battered her with his weapon. His clothes, if not his hands, would in this way be preserved.

I have said that it is of the first importance to trace who knew of the existence of the jewels, since this might greatly help the solution of the problem. In connection with this there is a passage in Lambie's evidence in New York which is of some importance. I give it from the stenographer's report, condensing in places:

Q. Do you know in Glasgow a man named —— ——?
A. Yes, sir.
Q. What is his business?
A. A book-maker.
Q. When did you first meet him?
A. At a dance.
Q. What sort of dance?
A. A New Year's dance. (That would be New Year of 1908.)
Q. When did you meet him after that?
A. In the beginning of June.
Q. Where?
A. In Glasgow.
Q. At a street corner?
A. No, he came up to the house at Prince's Street.
Q. Miss Gilchrist's house?
A. Yes, sir.
Q. That was the first time since the dance?
A. Yes, sir.

Q. Do you deny that you had a meeting with him by a letter
received from him at a corner of a street in Glasgow?

A. I got a letter.

Q. To meet him at a street corner?

A. Yes.

Q. The first meeting after the dance?

A. Yes.

Q. And you met him there?

A. Yes.

Q. And you went out with him?

A. No, I did not go out with him.

Q. You went somewhere with him, didn't you?

A. Yes, I made an appointment for Sunday.

Q. Did you know anything about the man?

A. Yes, I did, sir.

Q. What did you know about him?

A. I didn't know much.

Q. How many times did he visit you at Miss Gilchrist's house?

A. Once.

Q. Quite sure of that?

A. Quite sure.

Q. Didn't he come and take tea with you there in her apartment?

A. That was at the Coast.

Q. Then he came to see you at Miss Gilchrist's summer place?

A. Yes.

Q. How many times?

A. Once.

Q. Did he meet Miss Gilchrist then?

A. Yes, sir.

Q. You introduced him?

A. Yes, sir.

Q. Did she wear this diamond brooch?

A. I don't remember.

Q. When did you next see him?

A. The first week in September.

Q. In Glasgow?

A. Yes, sir.

Q. By appointment?

A. Yes.

Q. When next?

A. I have not met him since.

Q. And you say he only called once at the country place?

A. Once, sir.

Q. In your Glasgow deposition you say: "He visited me at Girvan and was entertained at tea with me on Saturday night, and at dinner on Sunday with Miss Gilchrist and me."

A. Yes, sir.

Q. Then you did see him more than once in the country.

A. Once.

[He read the extract again as above.]

Q. Was that true?

A. Yes.

Q. Then you invited this man to tea at Miss Gilchrist's summer house?

A. Yes.

Q. On Saturday night?

A. Yes.

Q. And on Sunday night?

A. He wasn't there.

Q. On Sunday you invited him there to dinner with Miss Gilchrist and yourself, didn't you?

A. Yes, sir. I didn't invite him.

Q. Who invited him?

A. Miss Gilchrist.

Q. Had you introduced him?

A. Yes, sir.

Q. He was your friend, wasn't he?

A. Yes, sir.

Q. She knew nothing about him?

A. No.

Q. She took him to the house on your recommendation?

A. Yes.

Q. Did she wear her diamonds at this dinner party?

A. I don't remember.

Q. You told him that she was a rich woman?

A. Yes.

Q. Did you tell him that she had a great many jewels?

A. Yes.

Q. Have your suspicions ever turned towards this man?

A. Never.

Q. Do you know of any other man who would be as familiar with those premises, the wealth of the old lady, her jewel-

lery, and the way to get into the premises as that man?
A. No, sir.
Q. Was the man you met in the hallway this man?
A. No, sir.

This is a condensation of a very interesting and searching piece of the cross-examination which reveals several things. One is Lambie's qualities as a witness. Another is the very curious picture of the old lady, the book-maker and the servant-maid all sitting at dinner together. The last and most important is the fact that a knowledge of the jewels had got out. Against the man himself there is no possible allegation. The matter was looked into by the police, and their conclusions were absolute, and were shared by those responsible for the defence. But is it to be believed that during the months which elapsed between this man acquiring this curious knowledge, and the actual crime, he never once chanced to repeat to any friend, who in turn repeated it to another, the strange story of the lonely old woman and her hoard? This he would do in full innocence. It was a most natural thing to do. But, for almost the first time in the case we seem to catch some glimpse of the relation between possible cause and effect, some connection between the dead woman on one side, and outsiders on the other who had the means of knowing something of her remarkable situation.

There is just one other piece of Lambie's cross-examination, this time from the Edinburgh trial, which I would desire to quote. It did not appear in America, just as the American extract already given did not appear in Edinburgh. For the first time they come out together:

Q. Did Miss Gilchrist use to have a dog?
A. Yes, an Irish terrier.
Q. What happened to it?
A. It got poisoned.
Q. When was it poisoned?
A. I think on the 7th or 8th of September.
Q. Was that thought to be done by someone?
A. I did not think it, for I thought it might have eaten something,

but Miss Gilchrist thought it was poisoned by some one.

Q. To kill the watch-dog — was that the idea?

A. She did not say.

The reader should be reminded that Slater did not arrive in Glasgow until the end of October of that year. His previous residences in the town were as far back as 1901 and 1905. If the dog were indeed poisoned in anticipation of the crime, he, at least, could have had nothing to do with it.

There is one other piece of evidence which may or may not have been of importance. It is that of Miss Brown, the schoolmistress. This lady was in court, but seems to have been called by neither side for the reason that her evidence was helpful to neither the prosecution nor the defence. She deposed that on the night of the murder, about ten minutes past seven, she saw two men running away from the scene. One of these men closely corresponded to the original description of the murderer before it was modified by Barrowman. This one was of medium build, dark hair and clean-shaven, with three-quarter-length grey overcoat, dark tweed cap, and both hands in his pockets. Here we have the actual assassin described to the life, and had Miss Brown declared that this man was the prisoner, she would have been a formidable addition to the witnesses for the prosecution. Miss Brown, however, identified Oscar Slater (after the usual absurd fashion of such identifications) as the second man, whom she describes as of "Dark glossy hair, navy-blue overcoat with velvet collar, dark trousers, black boots, something in this hand which seemed clumsier than a walking stick". One would imagine that this object in his hand would naturally be his hat, since she describes the man as bare-headed. All that can be said of this incident is that if the second man was Slater, then he certainly was not the actual murderer, whose dress corresponds closely to the first, and in no particular to the second. To the Northern eye, all swarthy foreigners bear a resemblance, and that there was a swarthy man, whether foreign or not, concerned in this affair would seem to be beyond question. That there should have been two confederates, one of whom had planned the crime while the other carried it out, is a perfectly feasible supposition. Miss Brown's story does not necessarily contradict that of Barrowman, as one would imagine that the second man would join the murderer at some little distance from the scene of the crime. However, as there was no cross-examination upon the story, it is difficult to know what weight to attach to it.

Let me say in conclusion that I have had no desire in anything said in this argument, to hurt the feelings or usurp the functions of anyone, whether of the police or the criminal court, who had to do with the case. It is difficult to discuss matters from a detached point of view without giving offence. I am well aware that it is easier to theorize at a distance than to work a case out in practice whether as detective or as counsel. I leave the matter now with the hope that, even after many days, some sudden flash may be sent which will throw a light upon as brutal and callous a crime as has ever been recorded in those black annals in which the criminologist finds the materials for his study. Meanwhile, it is on the conscience of the authorities, and in the last resort on that of the community, that this verdict, obtained under the circumstances which I have indicated, shall now be reconsidered.

Addendum

From *Who He? Goodman's Dictionary of the Unknown Famous* (Buchan & Enright, London, 1984):

After his experience with the Edalji case [see page 97], Conan Doyle had no wish to be involved in anything similar. But in 1910, following the appearance of *Trial of Oscar Slater*, edited by William Roughead and printed and published by William Hodge & Co. of Edinburgh as a title in the series of *Notable Scottish Trials*, he "went into the matter most reluctantly. . . . When I glanced at the facts, I saw that it was an even worse case than the Edalji one, and that this unhappy man had in all probability no more to do with the murder for which he had been condemned than I had."

With William Roughead and a Glasgow newspaper reporter named William Park, Conan Doyle sought to remedy the apparent miscarriage of justice; one of his first important actions was the publication in 1912 of a slim volume called *The Case of Oscar Slater*. Assistance came from an unexpected source: John Thompson Trench, a detective-lieutenant of the Glasgow police force, who had taken part in the murder investigation. He stated that, shortly after the discovery of the crime, Helen Lambie had told senior officers that the man she had seen leaving the flat was known to her: *known by name*, for he was one of Miss Gilchrist's most frequent visitors. For some reason, the officers involved had ignored this information; more than that, according to Trench, they had virtually dictated Lambie's written statement. Trench was ordered to disavow what he had said, and when he refused to do so, was dismissed from the force without a pension.

The name of the man referred to by Lambie (who in 1927, when she was living in America, confirmed Trench's statement) was never divulged in reports of hearings; nor, of course, in any of the several and diverse writings on the case by Conan Doyle, Roughead, and Park. Invariably, the letters A.B. were substituted. But since 4 July 1964, when the man died, aged eighty-eight, there has been no reason of law for keeping his identity secret. A scion of a wealthy Glasgow family, he was Dr Francis James Charteris; in the period around Marion Gilchrist's murder, he ran a general practice from his home in Great Western Road, close to the scene of the crime. In 1920 he was made professor of materia medica at St Andrew's University, where he remained until his retirement in 1948, having been for twenty years dean of the faculty of medicine.

I have said that in 1927 John Trench's statement was confirmed by Helen Lambie. This sparked off press activity, as a result of which another important prosecution witness, Mary Barrowman, recanted much of her evidence. Within a fortnight, Slater was released. The official announcement carried no suggestion that he had been wrongly convicted;

there was no mention of compensation for the eighteen and a half years he had spent in Peterhead Prison. Conan Doyle instigated, and guaranteed the costs of, an appeal within the High Court of Justiciary, Edinburgh. He must have experienced *déjà vu* of a most depressing kind when the appeal judges, like the commissioners in the Edalji affair, came up with a compromise decision — illustrating, it seemed to him, "the determination to admit nothing which inculpates another official". They concluded that the jury's verdict had been reasonable and that none of the new evidence affected the issue — but they discerned sufficient misdirection in the instructions given to the jury by the presiding judge Lord Guthrie (who was now dead) to warrant the setting aside of the verdict.

Slater received £6,000 as compensation. Directly after his discharge from prison, he had written a note of gratitude that began, "Sir Conan Doyle, you breaker of my shackels, you lover of truth for justice sake, I thank you from the bottom of my heart. . . ," but when Conan Doyle suggested repayment of money that he and others had spent during the long fight, Slater refused to part with a penny.

The Slater affair ended not with a bang but with rancour. Conan Doyle's final communication with the man he had helped to free was an abrupt note: "If you are indeed quite responsible for your actions, then you are the most ungrateful as well as the most foolish person whom I have ever known."

The Distribution of Hannah Brown

Anonymous

IN FEW INSTANCES has the public mind ever received so severe a shock as that produced by the discovery of the barbarous and revolting murder of which Greenacre was guilty. The mere mention of the name of this atrocious malefactor is a sufficient introduction to his case; and without further comment we shall proceed to describe the dreadful circumstances by which his crime was surrounded.

The first cause of suspicion of the murder having been committed arose from the discovery of the mutilated remains of a woman in the Edgware-road. It would appear that in the year 1836, some dwellings, called the Canterbury Villas, were in progress of completion, situated in the Edgware-road, at a distance of about a quarter of mile from the spot at which the Regent's Canal emerges from under the pathway. Five of these had been finished, and the gardens in front of them were protected from the public highway by a wall about ten feet high, which had not yet been extended to those houses in which the workmen were still employed. The materials for building lay along the side of the footpath, and in one of the finished houses, the only one which remained unoccupied by tenants, a man was lodged by the builder as a superintendent of the works, and as general watchman over the property which lay there. The severity of the weather towards the close of the month of December compelled the labourers to desist from work, and from Saturday the 24th of the month until the following Wednesday few persons visited the spot. On the latter day, 28 December, a man named Bond, a bricklayer engaged upon the buildings, visited his place of work; and about two o'clock in the afternoon was proceeding in the direction towards Kilburn, when his attention was attracted by his perceiving a package enveloped in a coarse cloth or sack, which appeared to have been carefully placed behind a paving-stone which was resting there, for the purpose of concealment. He removed the stone in order to obtain a more distinct view of the package, and was terrified to observe a pool of frozen blood, in such a position as exhibited that it had escaped through the wrapper of the parcel.

In a state of great alarm, he called the superintendent of the works, and another person, to the place, and they determined at once to open the package to ascertain the nature of its contents. Their astonishment and horror may easily be imagined, when they found that it consisted of a portion of the remains of a human body. The trunk only was there, the head and legs having been removed. Fearfully excited by this shocking discovery, they at once called in the aid of the police; and Pegler, a constable on duty, took charge of the dreadful package, and procured its immediate conveyance to the work-house of the parish of Paddington.

It was there at once submitted to the inspection of Mr Girdwood, the surgeon of the district, who made a most minute examination of all its parts. It proved to be the body of a female, apparently about fifty years of age, and who, from the appearances presented by the arms and hands, had evidently been employed in a laborious occupation. The head had been severed from the trunk in an awkward manner, the bone of the neck having been partly sawed through, and partly broken off; and the legs had been removed in a similar irregular way, the one at a distance of about four inches, and the other at a distance of about five or six inches, from the hip-joint. The body itself presented a healthy aspect, but exhibited a malformation of a peculiar nature, which eventually proved of material importance in proving its identification, but to which it would be indelicate more specifically to allude. The result of the investigation of Mr Girdwood, however, clearly showed that the deceased person had not met her death from any illness, and that therefore the presumption was that she had been murdered, and that the mutilation of her body had not taken place until subsequently to her decease, when, in all probability, means had been adopted by the murderer to conceal the identity of the person, as well as to dispose of her remains.

An occurrence of so extraordinary a nature, it may well be supposed, excited a degree of consternation and horror throughout the metropolis of the most fearful description; and the dreadful mystery in which the transaction remained wrapped for a considerable time, the remains of the deceased and her situation in life being alike unknown, tended in no small degree to extend the universal anxiety which prevailed. The body had been wrapped up in a piece of blue printed cotton, which appeared to have formed a child's frock, but which was worn to rags, an old towel, and part of a small white shawl, over which was placed a piece of sacking; but no marks were visible on either of the articles which could at all tend to afford any clue to their former possessor. Inquiries of the most minute and searching description were made with a view to ascertaining the means by which the mangled remains had been placed in the position in which they were found; and suspicion seemed to attach to a chaise-cart which had been seen to draw up near the spot on the previous Saturday night; but all the vigilance of the police failed, as well to discover the owners of this vehicle, as the murderer.

An inquest was held on the body on Saturday, 31 December, at the White Lion Inn, Edgware-road; but although every witness was examined, whose evidence tended to throw the smallest light on the occurrence, the jury were at length compelled to return a verdict of "Wilful Murder against some person or persons unknown". A minute description of the appearances and aspect of the body was then taken by Mr Girdwood; and in the course of the ensuing week, it was committed to the grave in Paddington churchyard, no prospect being yet afforded of the discovery of the remaining portions of the murdered woman's frame.

The public excitement, however, was soon afterwards wound to the very highest pitch, by a notification being given of the finding of a human head in a place called the "Ben Jonson Lock", of the Regent's Canal, which runs through Stepney fields. Universal credit at once attached it to the body which had been already discovered, and no time was lost in exhuming those remains, in order to ascertain the truth of the suspicions which were entertained.

This new discovery had been made on 7 January 1837, under circumstances of a remarkable character. A barge had entered the lock for the purpose of passing through it, and the lockman was engaged in closing the flood-gates at the tail of the lock, when he found that there was some obstacle which prevented their completely meeting. He remarked that he had no doubt that it was the carcass of a dead dog, and called to his assistant to bring him a long instrument called a hitcher, shaped like a boat-hook, usually employed for similar purposes, to remove it. Having made several ineffectual attempts to bring it to the surface of the water, he at length fixed his hitcher in the substance; and upon raising it from the water, it was seen to be the head of a human being. It was instantly brought on shore, and the circumstance communicated to the police, by whom the head was conveyed to Mr Birtwhistle, a surgeon, for examination.

His report stated that the face was disfigured with bruises and lacerations, and that the lower jaw was broken — injuries which were without doubt the result of the exertions of the lockman, first to close the gates, and secondly, to bring the head out of the water, but that there was appearance of a bruise on the eye inflicted during life; and further, that the head appeared to have been severed from the body in an awkward manner; the cervical vertebrae being sawed through in a rough way, evidently denoting that it had not been done by any surgeon. The exhumation of the body having now taken place, the necessary comparison was made, and Mr Girdwood at once declared that the head and the trunk were portions of the same frame.

Although some public satisfaction was afforded by this most singular event, still no clue whatever appeared yet to have been found to conduct the police to the murderer; for that murder had been committed there was no doubt. The expression of the face was so much altered and disfigured since the death of the woman that little hopes were entertained of

A *Famous Crimes* artist's impression of the discovery of Hannah Brown's head

the possibility of its identification. Thousands of persons inspected it, prompted by curiosity or a desire to secure the ends of justice, by pointing out the individual who had been murdered; and although frequent reports were circulated that the features had been recognized, no real evidence was obtained as to the person whose remains had been discovered. Decomposition in the head shortly commenced; and it was deemed advisable to adopt measures to prevent all remaining traces of the features being destroyed, and Mr Girdwood was instructed to take the necessary steps to secure this object. The head was accordingly placed in spirits, and was preserved at Mr Girdwood's, where it remained open to the inspection of all persons who it was supposed would be able to afford any information upon the subject.

The mystery which surrounded the case, however, seemed to become greater every day. The inquiries of the police for the remainder of the body were quite unsuccessful; and the difficulties which existed, arising from their total ignorance of the quarter to which their investigation should be directed, appeared to leave small hopes of its eventual dissolution. Until 2 February this obscurity still prevailed; but then accident again interfered to bring to light the remaining members of the body of the murdered woman.

On that day James Page, a labourer, was employed in cutting osiers in a bed belonging to Mr Tenpenny, in the neighbourhood of Coldharbour-lane, Camberwell, when in stepping over a drain or ditch, he perceived a large bundle lying in it, covered with a piece of sacking, and partly immersed in the water. His curiosity prompted him to raise it, and he saw what appeared to be the toes of a human foot protruding from it. He became alarmed and called for his fellow workman, who was only a short distance off; and upon their opening the package, they found it to contain two human legs. These, like the head, were transmitted to Mr Girdwood for examination, and proved to be portions of the frame which had been discovered in the Edgware-road.

Thus had three discoveries, each more remarkable than the last, produced the component parts of the body of the deceased; but the further interposition of the all-powerful hand of the Almighty was yet wanting to disclose the name and character of the murdered woman, as well as to point out her inhuman murderer. Intense anxiety was universally manifested by the public to unravel the mystery in which the dreadful transaction was enveloped; and every minute circumstance connected with the affair was sought after with the most astonishing avidity. Investigations of the most searching description were carried on by the authorities, but every inquiry proved fruitless.

That discovery which alone was wanting to satisfy the public mind was, however, at length made. On 20 March, Mr Gay, a broker residing in Goodge-street, Tottenham Court-road, applied to Mr Thornton, the churchwarden of the parish of Paddington, for permission to inspect such of the remains of the deceased woman as had been preserved above ground. He founded his application upon the fact of the sudden disappearance of his sister, whose name was Hannah Brown, and who having quitted her home on the afternoon preceding Christmas Day, had not since been seen or heard of. A request so reasonable was at once complied with; and upon Mr Gay seeing the head, which had been placed in spirits, he at once declared his belief that it was that of his unfortunate relation. Other persons who had been acquainted with Hannah Brown also came forward to express their opinion as to her identity; and from the statements which they made upon the subject of her habit of body, and the opinions which they expressed in reference to the identity of the head, no doubt remained of her being the individual who had been so inhumanly destroyed.

From the inquiries of the police, it was elicited that the unfortunate woman had received with favour the advances of a man named James Greenacre, to whom she was about to be married; and that on Christmas Eve she had quitted her lodgings in Union-street, Middlesex Hospital, in order to accompany her intended husband to his house, in Carpenter's-buildings, Camberwell, preparatory to their union on the ensuing Monday. Greenacre was the person in whose company she had been last seen; and to him, therefore, the authorities naturally turned for information, as to the manner in which they had parted, if they had parted at all, before her death. A warrant was granted by the magistrates of Mary-le-bone police-office for the apprehension of this man; and after considerable difficulty he was at length taken into custody on 24 March, at his lodgings at St Alban's-place, Kennington-road, together with a woman named Sarah Gale, with whom he cohabited, and her infant child.

On Monday, 25 March, an extraordinary degree of excitement prevailed throughout the parishes of Paddington and Mary-le-bone, in consequence of the apprehension of these persons being made known. At an early hour the greater part of High-street was thronged with persons who were anxiously awaiting the arrival of the prisoners. A coach was, at a quarter-past twelve o'clock, seen to approach the police-office, from which Greenacre and Mrs Gale were taken, and conducted through the magistrates' private entrance to the office. Upon their being placed at the bar, Greenacre appeared to be a man about fifty years of age, of middle height, and rather stout in figure. His aspect was forbidding, and he conducted himself with considerable firmness of demeanour. He was wrapped in a brown great-coat, and returned the gaze of any one who looked at him with an air of insolent bravado. Towards the close of the examination, however, he appeared to be oppressed with a sensation of weakness, a circumstance which was attributable to his having, during his sojourn in the station-house, attempted to strangle himself with his pocket-handkerchief — an attempt, the effects of which were only removed upon the introduction of surgical assistance.

The prisoner Sarah Gale was between thirty and thirty-five years of age; she was tolerably well dressed, and had with her a child between four and five years old; she seemed quite unconcerned at her situation, and was the object of as much, if not more, attention and interest as her fellow prisoner and paramour.

In the course of this and the succeeding examinations of the prisoners, evidence extending to a very great length was procured. A succinct narrative of the proceedings, however, will be perhaps better understood than a lengthy statement of the testimony of each particular witness; and to such a descriptive account, therefore, we shall confine ourselves.

The various witnesses having been examined, whose testimony was requisite to prove the circumstances attending the discovery of the body, the head, and the legs of the deceased woman, proof of the identity of those remains was given; and upon this subject the peculiarity of the formation of the body, to which we have already alluded, tended at once to dispel all doubts, if any such existed. Mrs Brown, it then appeared, had lived for about a year and a half before her death at No. 45, Union-street, Middlesex Hospital, where she gained a living by taking in washing and mangling. While in this situation she became acquainted with Greenacre, and the intimacy after a while ended in an offer of marriage on his part, which was accepted by her. Mr and Mrs Davis, of No. 45, Bartholomew-close, Smithfield, were friends of Mrs Brown, and were made acquainted by her with the nature of her connection with Greenacre; and they acceded to a proposition which was made to them, that Mr Davis should give away the bride, and that their daughter should act as bridesmaid. The day after Christmas Day was fixed upon as the day of the wedding, and the banns were in due course put up at the church of St Giles, Camberwell, preparatory to the nuptial rites.

On 22 December, Mrs Davis last saw Hannah Brown. The latter then called at her house with Greenacre, and they at that time appeared perfectly happy and "sociable", and, as it seemed, eagerly wishing for the wedding-day. They remained to supper and went away together, having immediately before their departure spoken of an intention which they had, after their marriage, to settle at Hudson's Bay.

On the afternoon of 24 December, Mrs Brown quitted her lodgings in Union-street, with Greenacre, in a coach, and on the same evening they were seen together at the residence of the latter, in Carpenter's-buildings. Mrs Brown had previously disposed of what little property she possessed; but as the coach would not contain all her personal movables, she took away the key of her door with her, saying that she would return for them at night. She did not return, however, and Mrs Corney (her landlady) did not again see her alive. On the night before Christmas Day, Greenacre called upon Mrs. Davis, and inquired whether she had seen anything of Hannah Brown? She answered that she had not; and Greenacre then said that he had found, upon enquiry, that Mrs Brown had deceived him as to her property, and that it would not do for them to

118

plunge themselves into poverty by marrying. At this interview he appeared agitated and angry, and his countenance presented an aspect of such peculiarity that it was remarked by Mrs Davis to her husband. On the Tuesday after Christmas Day, Greenacre called upon the brother of Mrs Brown; and he acquainted him also with the fact of the postponement of the marriage, saying that he and his intended wife had quarrelled with respect to her property, and that she had in consequence quitted his house, and he had seen nothing of her since.

In the meanwhile, the continued absence of Mrs Brown from her lodgings excited some apprehension in the minds of her friends; but it was not until 27 March (as we have already stated) that they exhibited any fears of the probability of the murdered remains which had been found being those of their unfortunate relative. An inspection of those remains, however, at once informed them of the melancholy cause of her disappearance.

The apprehension of Greenacre and Gale took place under circumstances which tended to confirm the suspicions of their guilt of murder, and to give conclusive evidence of their perfect cognizance of the fact of the death of the deceased. Inspector Feltham was the person by whom this capture was effected; and he took the prisoners into custody at a small house, No. 1, St Alban's-place, Kennington-road, accompanied by a police constable of the L division. He proceeded to that house and found them in bed together; and upon his entering the room, he informed them of the object of his visit. Greenacre at first denied all knowledge of any such person as Hannah Brown; but subsequently, upon his being further questioned, he admitted that he had been going to be married to her, although he did not then know what had become of her. The prisoners having dressed themselves, Greenacre declared that it was lucky that the officer had come on that night, for they were about to sail on the next day for America, a fact which appeared to be true, from the appearance of a number of boxes which stood in the apartment, ready packed and corded for travelling. A minute examination of the contents of the trunks afforded highly important evidence. Many articles were found

"I ARREST YOU FOR THE MURDER OF HANNAH BROWN

in them which were known to have belonged to Mrs Brown; but besides these, some remnants of an old cotton dress were discovered, exactly corresponding in pattern and condition with the pieces in which the body had been wrapped, on its being first seen in the Edgware-road.

Subsequent inquiries afforded additional proofs in the case, implicating both Mrs Gale and Greenacre. These consisted in the discovery of evidence as to the proceedings of the prisoners, on the night of Christmas Eve, and the following days. Greenacre, as we have already stated, was observed on Christmas Eve to take home his intended wife to his house in Carpenter's Buildings. Previously to this time, Mrs Gale had been living with him there as his wife; but she appears to have been sent away on the morning of 24 December, in order to make room for the newcomer. On that night some noise and scuffling was heard in Greenacre's house by the neighbours, but no notice was taken of it; and on the following day Greenacre was observed to go out, and the house remained locked up, and with the shutters closed all day. On that day it was proved that he went to dine with Mrs Gale, at lodgings which she occupied temporarily, at Portland-street, Walworth.

On Boxing Day (Monday), Mrs Gale was again in Carpenter's-buildings, and she seemed to be engaged in washing the house, as she procured some water from some of her neighbours, and she was noticed to be employed with a bucket and mop, as if she were hard at work. On Wednesday, Greenacre was observed to leave his home, carrying with him a blue merino bag, and it was ascertained that about a week afterwards he quitted the house in Carpenter's-buildings altogether, his boxes and furniture being removed by a man named Chisholm.

About a fortnight afterwards, the house was stated "to be to let", and several of the neighbours went to look at it. The floors of one or two of the rooms appeared to have been carefully scrubbed and cleaned; and besides this, there was observed to be a strong smell of brimstone, as if it had been employed in fumigating the house, and the fire-places were boarded up, so as to prevent the escape of the vapour by the chimney. Independently of these circumstances, various expressions were attributed to Greenacre and Mrs Gale, from which it was inferred that the latter was aware of the murder; and it was also shown that the bag or sack in which the body was enclosed had been stolen by Greenacre, about a week before Christmas, from the shop of a Mr Ward, a mangle-maker, in Cheyne-walk, Tottenham Court-road; whose shopman, Higgins, was enabled to identify it by a particular species of shaving, which was still adhering to its interior, and also by the cord, with which it was made to close.

Upon the statement of all these circumstances, the prisoners were called upon for any defence which they might have to make, and Greenacre thus addressed the magistrate. He spoke in a clear voice, and without betraying any emotion.

"I have to state that in the evidence given there are many direct falsehoods. I distinctly told Mrs Davis that we had had no words at all of consequence — that is, no quarrel. What I mentioned to her was that I had found out Mrs Brown had no money at all, and had tried to set up things in my name at a

James Greenacre

tally-shop. I merely argued the point with her, but there had been no dispute worth speaking of. There may have been duplicity on both sides. I represented myself to her to be a man of property, as many other people do; and I found out that she was not a suitable companion for me, which may fairly be concluded from her conduct towards her brothers and sisters. I'll adhere strictly to the truth in what I am saying, although there are many circumstances in the evidence combining together against me, and which may perhaps cost me my life. One of the witnesses has said that I helped to move the boxes on the Saturday; that is true, but I will precede that remark by stating that I had this female (the other prisoner) in a room at the time, where she was lodging, and did my cooking for me. I gave her notice to leave previous to Mrs Brown coming home, and she had left accordingly.

"On the Saturday night before Christmas Day, Mrs Brown came down to my house, rather fresh from drinking, having in the course of the morning treated the coachman, and insisted upon having some more rum, a quantity of which she had had with her tea. I then thought it a favourable opportunity to press upon her for the state of her circumstances. She was very reluctant to give me any answer, and I told her she had often dropped insinuations in my hearing about her having property enough to enable her to go into business, and that she had said she could command at any time three hundred or four hundred pounds. I told her I had made some inquiry about her character, and had ascertained she had been to Smith's tally-shop, in Longacre, and tried to procure silk gowns in my name. She put on a feigned laugh, and retaliated by saying she thought I had been deceiving her with respect to my property, by misrepresenting it. During this conversation she was reeling backwards and forwards in her chair, which was on the swing, and as I am determined to adhere strictly to the truth, I must say that I put my foot to the chair, and she fell back with great violence against a chump of wood that I had been using; this alarmed me very much, and I went round the table and took her by the hand, and kept shaking her, but she appeared to be entirely gone.

"It is impossible to give a description of my feelings at the time; and, in the state of excitement I was in, I unfortunately determined on putting her away. I deliberated for a little while, and then made up my mind to conceal her death in the manner already gone forth to the world. I thought it might be more safe that way than if I gave an alarm of what had occurred. No one individual up to the present moment had the least knowledge of what I have stated here. This female I perfectly exonerate from having any more knowledge of it than any other person, as she was away from the house."

Mrs Gale, after denying that she was at Camberwell at the time of the murder, or that she had participated in any way in causing the death of the deceased, said: "Mr Greenacre told me I was to leave his house a fortnight before Christmas, but I did not then leave, as I could not suit myself with lodgings, and

Sarah Gale

I went away on the following Thursday. On the Monday week after that I returned to the house, and he told me that the correspondence between him and Mrs Brown was broken off. That's all I have to state."

During the whole of the time occupied by the police in prosecuting their inquiries, new and increasing interest prevailed upon the subject of the case, and every opportunity was seized upon by the public at which it was thought that a glimpse of the prisoners might be obtained.

5 April was fixed upon for the last examination; but owing to the extreme difficulties which had attended every fresh inquiry before the magistrates at the police-office, arising from the crowds which were every day collected, they were induced to determine upon holding their final meeting at the New Prison, Clerkenwell, where Greenacre had been confined. Mrs

Gale had been kept in custody at the House of Correction; and the intention of the magistrates being soon made known to the mob, many of them proceeded from the neighbourhood of Mary-le-bone to Clerkenwell, in the hope of catching a glimpse of her as she passed to the New Prison. During the examination both prisoners were much affected, and trembled violently.

The principal object of this meeting was the re-perusal of the whole of the vast body of evidence which had been obtained in the presence of the prisoners. The statements made by Greenacre and his fellow-prisoner were also read, and signed by them as true. Gale, when called upon to affix her name to her statement, appeared to be labouring under extreme trepidation. She got up from her seat, and walked with a faltering step to the table; she took the pen with a trembling hand, when Greenacre, seeing the agitation she was in, said to her, "Sign, sign; don't frighten yourself at what people say about your going to be hanged, and all that sort of stuff!" Gale at length appended her name, and resumed her seat.

The whole of the evidence having now been read over, the prisoners were fully committed to Newgate for trial.

The following lines were circulated by Greenacre among the reporters present at this examination, with a view to their publication in the newspapers.

To a humane and enlightened public.
New Prison, Clerkenwell, April 5.

Everything that ingenuity and malice could invent to influence the minds of the ignorant, and to fill the minds of the good and religious with awe, has been the result of newspaper comment against me. It is said that the finger of God is manifested in bringing this horrid and wilful murder to light, the day only before my flight to America! I contend that this manifestation of Divine Providence is to serve my case, or the cause of a suffering mind, to prevent me from a life of continual dread of being fetched back from America upon this awful charge, and which would certainly have been the result, if the deceased had not been recognised until I had departed; thus it may be shown that Providence is on my side.

125

Again, if in my crossing the Atlantic, or by any other means, my death had ensued, the fatal conviction of an innocent female would certainly have been the result — suspicion would have been too strong against her to have saved her; it was for God, and God only, to prevent this fatal termination — no human mind could have discerned anything in her favour, if my death had preceded this investigation. God is just; and God be praised for this timely interference to prevent my premature death through either my crossing the seas, or the distracted state of my mind. I hope, therefore, that my unfortunate situation may not be prejudiced by malice and perverted comments.

Monday, 10 April 1837, was the day fixed for the trial of these offenders, and on that day they were placed at the bar of the Central Criminal Court, and arraigned upon the indictment found against them. Greenacre was charged, as the principal, with the wilful murder of the deceased, and Gale was indicted for being an accessory after the fact, in comforting, aiding, and assisting her fellow prisoner.

Chief Justice Tindal, Mr Justice Coleridge, and Mr Justice Coltman were the judges who sat to try these offenders, and the court was crowded in every corner.

The evidence produced now was a repetition of that which had been brought forward at the various examinations at the police-office. Mr Adolphus, Mr Clarkson, and Mr Bodkin appeared to conduct the case for the prosecution; and Mr Price and Mr Payne defended the prisoners. The line of defence was consistent with the statements which had been made by the prisoners at Mary-le-bone police-office. The witnesses who were competent to give any evidence as to the possibility of the truth of these declarations were cross-examined with a view to its being shown that Greenacre's account of the transaction might be correct; and further, that in the direction in which he stated Mrs Brown to have fallen, she might have passed through a doorway, which was behind her, and into the back-room. This suggestion was, however, negatived by the declaration of the witnesses; and the testimony of the surgeons who were examined also tended to prove that the injuries which had been received by the deceased could not have been the result of such a state of facts. Mr Girdwood underwent a long examination, and exhibited throughout an extensive acquaintance with those branches of his profession which were material to the inquiry. He declared his belief that many of the appearances of wounds or bruises on the head were the result of injuries inflicted during life; and, further, that the bloodless state of the arteries of the head exhibited that the process of disseveration had been commenced before life was extinct.

Mr Price addressed the jury for the prisoners, urging those topics in his argument to which he had applied himself on his cross-examination.

The Lord Chief Justice began to sum up at a quarter past six o'clock on the second day of the trial. Having recapitulated the terms of the indictment in form, his lordship proceeded to observe that the conviction of the prisoner Greenacre of murder or manslaughter would not necessarily involve the prisoner Gale in the charge, unless the jury were satisfied that the evidence was sufficient to bear out the allegation of her having been an accomplice in the transactions connected with the death of the deceased. He had no doubt the case would receive the most benevolent and patient attention of the jury. He would read over the evidence, and leave them to say whether they considered the prisoner Greenacre to have been the author of the woman's death, and whether the evidence amounted to proof of murder, or of manslaughter of an aggravated kind. There were certain undoubted principles of law which must be kept in mind. One was that where a person met his death from the hand of another person, that other person was bound, either by direct evidence or out of the circumstances of the case as they appeared in evidence before the jury, to mitigate or reduce the charge to the lower or minor class of offence. But then some circumstance of alleviation, mitigation, excuse, or justification must be brought before the court and jury, or be derivable by fair inference from the evidence. What they would have to say, therefore, was whether, looking at the whole of the case, they were satisfied that it was left on the broad ground on which it was started by the counsel for the prosecution — namely, the actual murder of the deceased individual — or whether there were any circumstances in the case to induce them to come to a conclusion of a milder character — namely, that of a felonious manslaughter or accidental homicide.

The learned judge then proceeded to refer to the evidence which had been adduced, commenting with great minuteness and perspicuity upon every circumstance from which the guilt or innocence of the prisoners was argued. He observed that the male prisoner had, by his own statement, admitted that he was guilty of manslaughter, unless they came to the conclusion that by an act of carelessness, or of playfulness in tilting up the chair, the woman had met her death. If, on the other hand, they were of opinion that the prisoner had occasioned the death of Hannah Brown, either by premeditated malice or by a malignity of feeling, caused by conduct of an exasperating nature, thereby giving rise to a spirit of revenge, then they must find him guilty of the higher offence. They would observe that the doctors had given it as their opinion that the knife had been applied to the neck during life; they would therefore have to say whether, being possessed of a malignant spirit, the prisoner had not taken the knife and completed that act which he had wickedly intended to effect.

He would exhort them to weigh well the circumstances of the case, which was one of extreme difficulty. Above all things, it behoved them to turn a deaf ear to any manifestations of clamour which might have been exhibited on the part of the public; such impressions ought at all times, but more especially upon an occasion like the present, to be banished from a court of justice. They would enter upon the performance of their solemn and painful duty with feelings of patience and calmness, giving to every portion of the evidence such favourable interpretation as it would allow, and they would give any benefit which might arise therefrom to the prisoners; they would look into all the evidence watchfully and narrowly, and if upon mature reflection they entertained a doubt of the guilt of the prisoner of the charge of murder, they would let him derive the full advantage and benefit of such a doubt. If, on the other hand, the evidence was so clear and satisfactory as that in their minds it brought the commission of the crime home to the prisoner, they would doubtless do their duty.

With respect to the other prisoner, Sarah Gale, if they found the male prisoner guilty, either of the crime of murder or manslaughter, they would say whether by her assistance and aid she had protected, comforted, and enabled him to screen himself from the justice of the country. If so, they would find her guilty of the charge for which she was indicted. If, on the other hand, they thought that she had not in any way acted as an accessory, and had had no guilty knowledge of the crime, then they would give her the benefit of such opinion, and return a verdict of acquittal.

The jury having retired from the box for the purpose of considering their verdict, after an absence of a quarter of an hour only, returned into court to deliver their decision upon the case.

As they passed to their box, Greenacre surveyed each of them with a keen, searching, and eager glance, as if to read in their expressions the fate which awaited him, and of which the jury were now the arbiters. His countenance, however, remained unchanged; and he still appeared to preserve the same degree of firmness and self-possession which distinguished his demeanour throughout the whole of the trial, and seemed as a man who had already anticipated his fate, and whose mind was made up to the worst that could befall him.

The prisoner Gale, on the contrary, seemed lost and bewildered, and almost unconscious of her awful situation; but with that feeling of attachment for her paramour which women will evince even under circumstances of misery, shame, and peril, she fixed her look during this painful interval of suspense and agony upon the countenance of him to whose fate she appeared to cling, even in this trying moment, when life or death was about to unite them once more, or sever their unfortunate connexion for ever.

The clerk of the arraigns, having called over the names of the jury, said, "Gentlemen, how say you: do you find the prisoner at the bar, James Greenacre, guilty or not guilty of the felony of murder with which he is charged?"

The foreman of the jury answered, "Guilty."

The question was then asked with regard to the prisoner Gale, and the foreman of the jury again answered: "Guilty."

The countenance of Greenacre remained unaltered. He exhibited no emotion, but leaned back in his chair and seemed perfectly indifferent to what might follow. Gale appeared almost unconscious of what was passing around her.

Upon the announcement of the result of the case outside the Court, the huzzaings of the crowd, who were impatiently awaiting its termination, were of the most deafening description; and several well-dressed persons were observed in elevated positions, waving their hats to the mob, as if upon the intelligence of some important victory.

The recent alteration in the law with regard to the period of the execution of murderers rendered it unnecessary that sentence should be immediately passed on the prisoners; but on the following day, 12 April, they were brought up to receive the judgment of the Court.

Upon their being called upon in the usual way, to say any thing they had to urge why sentence should not be pronounced upon them:

Greenacre (in a husky, but firm tone) said: "My Lord, my unhappy condition in this unfortunate affair has given rise to abundance of evidence against me, such as might be collected in any pot-house or gin-shop, owing to the reports spread abroad to my prejudice, upon which the jurymen have acted. It is contrary to reason and common sense to suppose that I should have meditated the death of the woman, much less that I should effect it in the manner described, because of the property she had. If that had been my object, I could have had it all on the next morning, when our marriage was to have taken place, and then it would have been mine. What, then, was my motive for murdering of her? It is —"

The Recorder: "This is all very proper matter to have been urged by your counsel at the trial, but should not be pressed upon the Court now. The only question now is, as to the matter of law. If there are the slightest grounds for questioning the verdict of the jury, your only course is to apply to the Secretary of State, the Court having no power of itself to interfere. Have you anything more to say?"

Greenacre: "In the next place, my Lord, I beg to say that this woman was utterly ignorant of the affair up to the time of my being taken to the police-office. She had no knowledge whatever of it, and is as innocent as any lady or gentleman in this court. This I say, as I am going into my grave — that she is innocent. I invited her back to the house after the body was removed, and she never knew anything of it. I deem it a religious duty to exculpate her from having any concern in this unfortunate affair. I have no more to say."

The Recorder: "I shall make the same observation to you, Gale, that I have just addressed to the other prisoner. If there be any ground for a further inquiry into your case, you must apply to the Secretary of State, who will exercise his best discretion upon the subject, under the advice of the responsible officers of the Crown."

The prisoner Gale was then led to a chair at the back of the dock, and the usual proclamation for silence, preparatory to the passing of the sentence of death, having been made, —

The Recorder, in a solemn and impressive tone, proceeded to address the male prisoner in the following words: "James Greenacre, after a protracted trial, which endured for two entire days, upon a patient and impartial investigation of all the circumstances connected with your case, a jury of your country have found themselves inevitably compelled to find you guilty of the dreadful offence for which you were indicted. You have been convicted upon evidence, indeed the most satisfactory, of the crime of wilful murder. The appalling details of your dreadful case must be fresh in the recollection of all who now hear my voice, and will long live in the memory and (may I not add?) in the execration of mankind; and generations yet to come will shudder at your guilt. You have, indeed, acquired for yourself a revolting celebrity: an odious notoriety in the annals of cruelty and crime.

"The means to which you were prompted to resort, in order

to conceal the mangled and dismembered portions of your victim, were for a season attended with partial success. You disposed of her remains, as you thought, in places secure from discovery, but that course availed you not; for after a short interval accumulated evidence and irrefragable proofs of your guilty contrivance became apparent. The amputated limbs and the dissevered body were united to the bloodless head of the murdered woman, and every injury by you inflicted after death has afforded the means of proving by comparison, beyond doubt, that the wound on the eye was inflicted by you while your victim was in life, and strength, and health. Horrible and revolting to humanity as was the spectacle presented by the mutilated trunk and mangled remains, fresh details and discoveries suggested both the means and manner by which you accomplished the destruction of the deceased. Both surgical skill and medical science came to the assistance of common observation; and it was clearly and beyond all doubt demonstrated that the wounds on the eye and skull were sufficient to produce death; and it was still further proved that while the blood was yet in a fluid state, and circulating through the veins and arteries, you accomplished your horrible object, by severing the head from the body. Stupor of the senses and suspended animation were the effect of your blows; and then you imbrued your hands in the gushing life's-blood of the wretched and unhappy being who was stretched senseless and unconscious at your feet. The still warm corpse was then barbarously mutilated and mangled by you, in the hope that the eye of man would not detect your guilt; but the eye of God was upon you. The natural disgust and horror which your conduct in this respect excites, compels me to throw a veil over the frightful and appalling particulars of that hideous scene.

"But even that scene, revolting as it is, may be useful in a moral point of view, for it shows how the hand of Providence points out the guilty, and proves both the means of detection and the certainty of punishment. The certain but unseen agency of Providence is exhibited in the development of the peculiar and complicated circumstances of your case. The curiosity excited, the alarm produced, and the peculiarity of each succeeding discovery of the mangled members of the body, and the seemingly impenetrable mystery in which the circumstances of such a murder were shrouded, all conspired to awaken suspicion, renew inquiry, and incite to fresh exertion, until at last the mystery was developed by the family of the deceased. The embalmed head was identified, the name of the murdered woman came to light, and sufficient evidence was produced to point out you as the author of her death, and bring you before the tribunal of public justice. The circumstances attending the discovery of this murder lead to the inevitable conclusion that neither cunning nor ferocity can shelter and secure a murderer; for although the crime may be hidden for a time — although delays may occur, and the mystery of the transaction almost preclude the hope of its discovery, yet the all-seeing eye of God is cognizant of the deed, and man becomes the agent of its discovery. Indeed, instances of escape from such a crime are so rare that the detection is almost as sure as the punishment is certain.

"It is plain from the attention with which I perceive you are listening to what I now say that I am addressing an individual not devoid of education, of reasoning faculties, and strength of mind. The occasion you must indeed be aware is, as regards yourself, standing where you do, and under the circumstances in which you are placed, awful and solemn to the last degree, both as regards your fate in this world and the world to come. I will not draw arguments from my own feeble resources alone, to endeavour to induce and implore you to repent before it is too late. Let me, then, before I proceed to pass upon you the dreadful sentence, entreat you to consider well your past life, and the chances which await you in the life which is to come. . . . The limits of time and the span of this present life furnish no obstacles in the way of a repentant sinner. Turn, therefore, I implore you, with an humble and penitent heart, to the source of all hope and mercy — the blessed Redeemer of mankind — and employ the brief interval which is yet left you on this side of eternity in penitence and prayer, as the only means of obtaining that mercy hereafter which the laws of God and man deny to you in this world.

"It now only remains for me to pass upon you the dreadful sentence of the law; and that sentence is, that you be taken from hence to the prison from which you came, and from thence to a place of execution, where you shall be hanged by the neck until you are dead, and that your body be then buried within the precincts of the jail; and may the Lord God Almighty take compassion on your sinful soul."

The learned Recorder towards the end of this address was sensibly affected; and he could scarcely give utterance to the concluding words.

The prisoner Greenacre remained apparently unmoved, but he listened with attention, and never once changed his position or relaxed a muscle. He was then led back, and

Gale was brought forward to receive her sentence.

The Recorder said: "Sarah Gale, I will not aggravate the sufferings which you must now endure with any observations tending to increase those sufferings. The unhappy man who a short time ago stood beside you at that bar has declared that you had no guilty knowledge of the transaction in which he was involved. I cannot but observe, however, with regard to that remark, that you had united yourself to him, sharing his society and bed, and comforting, assisting, and sheltering him, without being joined to him by any moral or religious tie. As he has stated that you were ignorant of the dreadful transaction, I think it right to remind you that the earrings found in your pocket had belonged to the unfortunate woman who had been slaughtered by his hands; that duplicates of property which belonged to her were also found in your possession; and that in an adjoining room a box was found, proved to have been hers, besides other property.

"I cannot, therefore, as at present advised, entertain any doubt but that the verdict of the jury in your case was well and justly grounded. How far your attachment to the prisoner induced you to continue your intercourse with him, notwith-standing his possession of the property of the deceased under circumstances which I should think must at least have excited suspicion in your mind, it is not for me to judge. Perhaps you considered that what had been done could not be undone; but whatever feeling actuated your conduct in connexion with the circumstances of the case, I feel that I am bound to pass upon you the full sentence directed by the act of parliament; and if upon further investigation of your case, should you be disposed to apply to the Secretary of State for a revision of your sentence, any favourable circumstances should arise, that matter will be considered and disposed of by the competent authorities.

"At present I have only to pronounce upon you the sentence of the law; and that sentence is, and this Court do adjudge, that you be transported beyond the sea to such place as His Majesty, with the advice of his privy council, shall direct and appoint, for the term of your natural life."

The prisoners were then led away from the bar; but Greenacre, instead of being conducted to the condemned cell, as is customary, was re-taken to the apartment which he had previously occupied. The reason for this alteration in his case was the necessity which existed for a strict watch being maintained over him, to prevent a repetition of the attempt which he had made upon his own life, which there was good reason to apprehend; and it was felt that the inclemency of the weather would render such a duty, in the lower cells of the prison, a punishment upon the attendant turnkeys of no ordinary severity.

The demeanour of Greenacre, after his conviction, partook of the same firmness and determination which he had hitherto maintained; and upon the day after his condemnation he requested to be supplied with pens, ink, and paper. His desire was instantly complied with; and from this time he appeared to be occupied in the fabrication of a new statement, bearing the impress of truth, in reference to the foul crime for which he had been tried. He industriously applied himself for several days to this task; but none of the productions of his pen appeared to afford him satisfaction, and each was committed to the flames almost immediately upon its completion.

In the course of the day after he received sentence of death, he was visited by the sheriffs, and to them he made a new confession of the circumstances of his crime. The general facts which he now detailed corresponded with the story he had told at the police-office; but in one most important particular he admitted the falsehood of that statement. This was with reference to the immediate cause of the death of Mrs Brown; and he now stated that the unfortunate woman, having accompanied him home, as proved in evidence, they had taken tea together. Mrs Brown afterwards proceeded to wash up the tea-things, and while she was so occupied, they continued a conversation which had before commenced, upon the subject of her property. He became enraged at the deception which she had practised on him, and seizing a rolling-pin which lay on the dresser, he menaced her with it, and at length struck her on the eye. She fell to the ground, and on his going to her, he was shocked to find that she was insensible, and apparently dead. He paced the room for some time, in terror at the act which he had committed, as he conjectured that he should be charged as her murderer, and began to reflect upon the best means of screening himself from the consequences of his guilt.

A variety of methods presented themselves to his mind; but at length he hit upon the horrible expedient of dividing the limbs from the body, and disposing of the dissevered members separately. He, in consequence, immediately set about cutting off the head, and having done so, he suffered the whole of the blood to drain from it. This done, he determined instantly to get rid of this portion of the frame of his victim, and wrapping it in a silk pocket-handkerchief, he quitted the house with the horrible burden. On reaching Camberwell he got into an omnibus, which conveyed him to Gracechurch-street, and without alarm for the discovery of the contents of his bundle, he carried it on his knee during the whole journey. When he left the vehicle he scarcely knew which way to turn, but a Mile-End omnibus overtaking him as he reached Cornhill, he jumped into it, and was conveyed to the East end of the town, still carrying his dreadful load on his lap, in the same manner in which he had supported it before. On his leaving this second conveyance, he walked on until he reached the Regent's Canal, and he pursued the course of it until he came to the Lock at Stepney. An idea suddenly suggested itself to his mind, that this was the fitting place to get rid of the head, and without more ado he "shot it from the handkerchief into the water". He then directly turned back, and on his way home he called at Mrs Davis's, in Bartholomew-close, with whom he entered into conversation, as described in the evidence. He slept in Carpenter's-buildings alone on that night, but on the morning he went to Mrs Gale's lodgings, where he staid until the next day.

At an early hour on the morning of 26 December, he proceeded to his own house, to dispose of the remaining parts of the body. He began by separating the legs from the trunk, and having done so, he packed them up in a sack and took them to Coldharbour-lane (it being quite daylight at the time), and threw them into the osier bed. He then once more resumed his dreadful task at his house, in Carpenter's-buildings, the trunk of the body being now all that he had to get rid of. The sack and the remnants of a gown which were discovered with the body were the only coverings in which he could wrap these remains, and having securely corded them up, he took the bundle on his back and went out, undetermined as to the course which he should pursue to dispose of this remaining evidence of his guilt. A carrier's cart passed him soon after he reached the public road, and his load being heavy, he requested permission to place it on the tail-board. This was acceded to, and he walked behind the cart as far as the Elephant and Castle, at Newington. The carrier there stopped to procure his dinner, and left him in the street to take care of the cart; but alarmed lest, during the prolonged absence of the driver, some accident might occur which should procure his detection, he called a hackney cab, and having thrown his bundle under the seat, directed that he should be driven to the Edgware-road.

On his arrival at the Pine Apple Gate, he quitted the vehicle, and paid the driver, and the man having turned back, he walked on towards Kilburn. A favourable opportunity soon presented itself for disposing of the load, and he deposited it behind the stone in the position in which it was found two days afterwards. This also, he declared, took place in the day-time, and he conceived that he underwent less risk in pursuing his operations thus openly than in endeavouring to conceal them under the shades of night. On his return home, he burned the handkerchief in which he had carried the head, and he also wiped up the blood from the floor with flannels, which he disposed of by throwing them down the privy.

This confession was not reduced to writing; but the evident object of the prisoner was to screen Mrs Gale from the punishment which awaited her, and to raise a belief of her innocence. This, however, failed, for the evidence which was adduced with reference to her implication in the murder was too clear to admit of any doubt being entertained; and indeed the general impression was that the murder was the result of a pre-conceived determination, both of Greenacre and his paramour, in order to the accomplishment of which by the former, the latter only temporarily quitted his house.

During the subsequent imprisonment of Greenacre, he appeared to be little anxious for the spiritual consolation of the reverend gentleman who was the ordinary of the jail. He occasionally employed himself in the perusal of religious works, but was generally engaged in writing, although the result of his labours in this respect were, as we have already stated, usually burned. In the conversations which he had with the official persons by whom he was visited, he complained loudly of the prejudices which had been excited against him by the circulation of a great many false accounts of circumstances which had occurred in his early life. He particularly referred to an allegation which had been made, of his having murdered one of his children, of which Mrs Gale was the mother; and he asserted, and Mrs Gale corroborated the truth of his declaration, upon her being separately questioned, that the child had died a natural death; although he admitted that he had disposed of it, by placing it at the door of a Mr Dale, in Rupert-street, Haymarket, by whom it was sent to St James's Workhouse, where it lived for nine months.

On Wednesday, 26 April, the case of Greenacre was reported to His Majesty by the Recorder, and the following Tuesday, 2 May, was fixed for the execution. The intelligence was on the same evening conveyed to the prisoner, but he seemed to have made up his mind to the impossibility of there being any mitigation in his punishment, and was unmoved. He declared that he cared nothing for death, although he was sacrificed to the prejudices of the world; but he shuddered at the thought of quitting life with the brand upon him of a wilful murderer. He maintained that he had committed no murder, and that he was to blame for nothing except the mutilation of the body of the deceased. At his meeting now with the ordinary, he declined his spiritual assistance, and said that he could find no relief in anything but inward prayer.

On the following Sunday, the condemned sermon was preached in the chapel of the jail by Dr Cotton, and the most intense anxiety was exhibited on the part of the public to procure admission to this ceremony. Greenacre throughout the service conducted himself with much propriety, and repeated the responses with accuracy and precision. During the sermon, however, in which he was spoken of as a murderer, he appeared to be much incensed; and on his being subsequently visited by the worthy ordinary, he complained of the application of that term to him, and not without warmth, he declared that he thought the observations which had been made might have been spared. Subsequently, however, he resumed his wonted composure, and he appeared to receive the attentions of the clergyman with more satisfaction. On Monday night he was requested to join the ordinary in partaking of the sacrament, but he declined to do so; and in the course of a conversation which passed upon the subject, he asserted that although he believed that the Saviour was a very good man, he placed no credit in the assertion that he was the Son of God. To further questions which were put to him, he said that he believed in the existence of a Deity, and in a future state of rewards and punishments, but that he had no doubt that he should be happy, for the sufferings through which he had passed in life were a sufficient atonement for any faults of which he had been guilty.

On Monday night he slept soundly for several hours; but about four in the morning he arose and dressed himself, and indited several letters. He had completed these by seven, and at that hour he partook of some refreshment, and now, for the first time since he had entered Newgate, he was observed to shed tears. As the hour of eight approached, his agitation increased, but he remained absorbed in silent meditation. Upon the appearance of the usual officers, he submitted with calmness to the operation of pinioning; and this being completed, he requested as a favour, that he might not be long exposed to the gaze of the multitude without. The last words which he uttered conveyed a request that his spectacles might be given to Sarah Gale; and then, unheeding the remarks of Mr Cotton, he joined the procession to the scaffold.

The exterior of the jail meanwhile presented a wondrous scene of confusion. The mob had begun to collect as early as ten o'clock on the night before, and at day-break on Tuesday morning, every spot was occupied from which a glimpse of the scaffold could be obtained. At four o'clock the erection of the scaffold was commenced; and the appearance of this instrument of death, as it was wheeled from the prison-yard, was hailed with three cheers of deafening applause. The same terrible welcome was given, at a subsequent period, to the transverse beam when it was raised above the platform; and again to the executioner, when he came forward to fasten the deadly halter on the chain which is suspended from it.

The pressure of the crowd as the hour of execution approached became terrific; and many persons were carried from it, exhausted by their exertions. At a quarter before eight the bell of St Sepulchre's Church began to toll, and from that moment the screams and groans occasioned by the pressure from the two extremities of the crowd towards the centre were perfectly appalling. When the executioner again presented himself on the scaffold, however, to see that all the preparations were complete, every feeling seemed to give way to that of curiosity; but it became evident that there was a sensation in that immense assemblage, which would express itself in clamorous exultation as soon as ever the wretched criminal appeared, to atone for the blood which he had so unrelentingly shed. No sooner did those officers who usually precede the criminal to the place of execution become visible than it burst forth with a loud, deep, and sullen shout of execration against Greenacre, even before that miserable wretch came under the terrible ordeal of their indignant glance.

As soon as he mounted the scaffold, the populace again exhibited their detestation of the bloody atrocity of which he had been convicted, by setting up a wild hurrah of approval of the retaliation which he was about to endure under the hands of the ministers of justice. He placed himself at once in the hands of the executioner, who was thus enabled to complete the final preparations for his death with unprecedented rapidity. The ordinary then read the commencing verse of the burial-service, and before it was concluded the bolt was withdrawn, Greenacre fell, and the vengeance of the law was accomplished. In two minutes from his first appearance on the platform he ceased to be a living man. One grasp of his hands was observed on the rope reaching its full tension — nothing more, and then all was still.

In a few minutes afterwards the mob began to disperse; but a large concourse of persons remained until nine o'clock, when the body was cut down amidst a yell of triumph, which will live long in the memory of those who heard it. On the same night the body of the criminal was buried within the precincts of the jail, near to those of Thistlewood and others, who had been executed for high-treason.

Gale, it may be observed, during the latter part of her imprisonment, previously to the time of the execution of her late paramour, fell into a state of great despondency. She had been informed that an interview with Greenacre could not be permitted; and this, combined with the certainty of his death, and her apprehensions as to her own fate, reduced her to a state of the greatest mental weakness. The wretched woman, after some delay produced by the applications of her friends in her behalf, was, on 26 June, removed from Newgate to the Hulks, whence eventually, accompanied by her child, she was transported.

Having now related the particulars of this atrocious case, we

LIFE, TRIAL, AND EXECUTION
OF JAMES GREENACRE,

With a Copy of a Letter addressed to Mrs. Greenacre in America.

INTERIOR OF THE

CHAPEL OF NEWGATE.

This man after a lengthened Trial, which lasted two days, viz. the 10th and 11 days of April, the particulars of which we gave in former publications, was found guilty of the Wilful Murder of Hannah Brown, to whom, as was supposed, he was to have been married

The only confession he made as can possibly be relied on, was as follows, though he had private communications with Mr. Cotton, and Mr. M'Murdo, the Chaplin and Surgeon of Newgate.

When the Recorder had passed sentence upon Greenacre, he appeared to be very uneasy, and asked to see one of the turnkeys, he was accordingly waited on, when he stated, that when himself and Mrs. Brown entered his apartments in Carpenters Buildings, they had words concering the deception that had been resorted to, by both parties, when she being very agrievating, he took up a piece of wood, resembling a jack-towel-roller, and gave her a blow over the eye ; she was then in the act of falling, but caught her and placed her in a chair, then took a knife and ran it across her throat, and placed a pail by her side to catch the blood. He then sat down to consider in what way he should dispose of the body ; many plans occured to him, but he decided on cutting it up, and disposing of it any way possible. He severed the head and legs from the trunk, and carried the head to Mrs. David in Bartholomew-close, (who in her evidence it will be remembered stated that Greenacre had a bag with what she supposed to be a quarterly loaf in it), where he stoped until about 11 o'clock on the same evening as the deed was committed, (Christmas-eve), and then hastened on to

Stepney, and threw it in the Regent's-canal, near the locks. He could then proceed no father, but protested to the innocence of Gale.

LETTER,
Chapel Yard, Newgate,
April 30, 1837.

Dear Louisa,

I am sorry you should have to upbraid me with having forgotten the duties of a husband, but assure you from the hour I took my farewell of you, (which was then my intention to have been but for a short period), through the treachery of those who termed themselves friends, I have been involved in difficulties, which has at length proved a fatal result, some idea of which you may form by noticing from whence this is directed.

There is no occasion, dear girl, for me to enter into the particulars concerning the cause of my lamentable end, as you will, if you have not already, through the medium of the press, which has, in every particular, endeavoured to blacken my character, undeservedly. However, I freely forgive all, as I hope to be forgiven, not only by man, but by my Almighty God, to whom, I hope, you will fervently pray on my behalf.

Receive, dear girl, the blessing of your ilsated and forlorn Husband.

JAMES GREENACRE.

P.S. Long ere this reaches you, I shall be no more.

EXECUTION.

This morning, at a very early hour, the houses facing, and all the avenues leading to the goal, were crowded with persons anxiously awaiting the fatal time which would assuredly terminate this wretched man's wicked career. At a quarter to 8 o'clock, the hangman appeared on the gallows, and prepared the rope, noose, &c, and at 8 o'clock, the Prisoner, attended by the Sheriff, and Chaplin, came forward in solemn procession, and was then shortly launched into eternity.

Printed and Published by J. V QUICK, Bowling Green Lane, Clerkenwell.

shall proceed to lay before our readers the sketch which Greenacre himself published of his life, during the period of his incarceration. It was in the following terms, and, as will be seen, was written before his trial:

Having furnished my counsel and legal advisers with every true and particular statement of my case, I conceive it to be my necessary duty towards myself, my family, and a reflecting public, to pen a brief outline of my history, in the hope of counteracting the vindictive feeling and public prejudice which have been excited against me, through falsehood and exaggerated statements that have appeared in the public newspapers, and which it is my duty to refute, by immediately committing this narrative to paper, to prove to the world that I am not that bloody-minded character which is reported of me, to the prejudice of my character in the minds of those persons in whose hands my life is placed.

I am not immaculate; neither am I without many sins of commission and omission; but that truth may appear, and that justice may be done to my name when I am no more, should the prejudice of my jury prevail over the extenuating facts of my case, I proceed to state the circumstances of my life.

I was born in 1785, in Norfolk [at a village called Westwinch, two miles and a half from Lynn, we believe], of honest and industrious parents, who were farmers. I only, of a large family, relinquished the business of a farmer, and was put into business in the grocery line, in the parish of St George, in the Borough, by my own parents, at the age of nineteen. From the moment I became a landlord, no tenant of mine ever questioned the kindness of my disposition; I have been many years in the possession of three cottages, which I built in Jane-place, Old Kent-road, and have had many tenants, but never distrained upon any of them for rent, but have always taken pleasure in assisting them in any difficulty, and have often, very often, given up to them their back rents or arrears that unavoidably happen to poor persons in cases of sickness, and the want of employment. I had also eight cottages in Bowyer-lane, Camberwell, but I never once distrained upon a tenant in my life, but have absolutely felt all the sympathy of a near relative, when my claim for rent has been met by an apology through sickness, in times of accouchement, and other causes of distress. I can with perfect safeness say, that of these eleven cottages, and those two in Carpenter's-place, I never distrained upon a poor tenant in my life.

Now, as regards my domestic history, I will just refer to a few demonstrations of my disposition and general character, as a husband, a father, and a respected friend. I have been a man of affliction, in losing three amiable companions, with whom I always lived in the most perfect harmony. It may be added, that I was no fortune-hunter in these cases; but I always sought after the prospects of my issue, by forming an alliance where my children might reap the advantages of their mother's dower on the death of their parents; and I have much consolation in finding that my children, by each of my wives' parents, are amply provided for by legacies. Before I pass over this trait in my character as a husband and father, the scandalous reports of my enemies make it necessary to refer to the deaths of my wives.

The first was the daughter of Charles Ware, of the Crown and Anchor Tavern, Woolwich, to whom I was married at the age of nineteen; my wife eighteen. I was then in business in the grocery line, by the assistance of my own parents, who were farmers in Norfolk. My wife died suddenly of a putrid sore throat. She was attended by that eminent physician, Dr Blackburn, who, and whose assistants, admonished me not to go near my wife to receive her breath; but such being the result of my feelings, that I could not resist the force of affection, and there are many persons now living who can bear testimony to the fact, I took the complaint, and it nearly cost me my life. I engaged a respectable woman as housekeeper, who, as nurse and housekeeper, has since been in my service at intervals for a period equal to thirteen years, and who is now living. My next wife was the daughter of Mr John Romford, a considerable land-owner in Essex. By this lady I also had two children. This wife died of a brain fever, brought on by exerting herself, I believe, riding on horseback, whilst on a visit at her own relations; and having an infant at the time, her milk was affected by the fever, which caused her death. Mr Culthred, now residing in the Borough, attended her. My old housekeeper, who nursed my wife at each accouchement, now became my housekeeper again. I continued a widower fifteen months, and married Miss Simmonds, of Long-lane, Bermondsey, with whom I also lived in harmony and affection up to the time I went to America (May 1833). This amiable companion, with whom I had arranged to come after I had provided a home for her, died in London of the cholera, about three weeks after my departure. By this wife I had seven children, two only of whom are living. My old housekeeper always attended as nurse to all my wives, and upon all occasions of sickness, making a period of near thirteen years. As a sober and affectionate husband, no person living can deny but this has uniformly been my character. I have always abhorred a public-house, and the babble of drunken men. The society of my books, and wife, and children, have always been to me the greatest source of delight that my mind could possibly enjoy.

As a master and a friend, I trust the following statement will show that kindness and liberality, and a desire to cultivate the friendship of my neighbours and the tranquillity of my home, have always been the object of my study, and a pleasure most dear to my heart. My apprentices and servants have always manifested much pleasure in their situations, and have always continued with me several years. My apprentices have always been the sons of respectable persons, and have generally been the means of recommending each other, through their connections with each other's families. I always received a good premium with each apprentice, one only excepted, who was a cast-off apprentice from the Foundling, but who became a good servant under a kind master and mistress, and staid with us many years after her apprenticeship was expired. I have had seven male apprentices since I commenced business, in 1814. Two were brothers, the sons of Mr Falls, who was then measurer in His Majesty's dockyard, Deptford; and my last apprentice, in 1833, was the son of Mr Green, of the Royal Oak, Sevenoaks, in Kent, whose eldest son had served his time, five years, with me, and with whom I received a large premium. I have always encouraged my servants and apprentices by very many indulgences and kind treatment, and have always found them obliging and assiduous in business. I had one who robbed me. This was the son of a highly respectable tradesman in London. I gave the boy in charge of the beadle, and, contrary to my wishes, he was remanded to Horsemonger-lane jail. I applied to the youth's father, to consult upon his son's escape. This gentleman's tears and distress of mind I most acutely participated in, and had near been brought into trouble by refusing to prosecute. No servant or inmate of my house can say that I was ever intoxicated, or that I ever lifted my hand against my wife, or caused a tear by harsh treatment.

Now, as a friend, I think I can give the most incontrovertible testimony; and had it not been for the infamous lying and slandering newspapers, who glory in any crime for the sale of their dangerous weapons, I might have received the visits, advice, and assistance of hundreds of friends, but all are frightened by those horrifying falsehoods. I have received anonymous letters whilst in jail, which I have shown to the governor of the prison, and have handed to my solicitor, wherein the writers express their wishes to aid me, but durst not avow their names. My counsel also have received instructions to aid me by the receipt of anonymous letters enclosing money, with the like expressions of the writers' fear that their names may be known. Thus it is that I am compelled to give this brief outline of my life, in the hopes of defeating the power of falsehood and slander.

I have continued in business twenty years in the parish of St George, in the Borough. I have always lived under the same firm, or landlord, and have always experienced an increasing connection of customers and friends. This manifestation of friendship was evinced by my numerous fellow parishioners in their electing me to the office of overseer, on Easter Tuesday, 1832, by the largest vestry that ever assembled in the parish church of St George. A poll was demanded, and my friends increased, and never before or since have there been so many parishioners polled. These numerous parishioners, with whom I had resided so many years, would now most willingly aid me by a subscription or other means, but that they are naturally frightened by the false and slanderous newspaper reports.

As a debtor, when in business, no person was ever more punctual in his payments; and at the time I went to America, my debts, about £150, were never before so trifling, and the number of my creditors were so few, I had left with my wife the invoices and the cash to pay them; but her illness and sudden death by the cholera caused the discharge of those bills to be neglected, when my creditors, who knew that I had houses, and who, misconstruing the cause of their not being called upon, proceeded by combining their small accounts to make me a bankrupt. Never before, I believe, was a person made a bankrupt whose debts were so trifling as mine. Had fraud been my object in going to America, I could have easily had ten times the debts and as many more creditors, with whom I had dealt for many years. I have one creditor only who has refused to sign my certificate, and from him I never demanded a stamp receipt, which has saved him a sum nearly equal to the debt I owed him.

I have mentioned my abhorrence of public-houses; I trust,

therefore, that the vice of drinking, the foundation of error and crime, may not be considered the cause of my unhappy accident and subsequent resolve to put away the body, which has produced my disreputable notoriety. It was the horror of my feelings, and fear only, that took possession of my mind. I was actuated by no feelings of a felonious or malicious kind. The unfortunate deceased was evidently very much in liquor when her chair went backwards; and had candidly avowed her poverty when I talked to her on the consequences of our marrying in deception, and of her having been to a tally-shop to obtain a dress upon credit in my name. Felonious intentions cannot be attributed to me, since it is well known that if she had property it might have been mine in a few hours' time by the legal right of marriage.

With reference to this autobiography, there is no reason to believe that any of the main facts which are stated are incorrect, but it appears that throughout his life Greenacre had been notorious among his acquaintance for the violence of his political opinions, and the unreserved manner in which he stated them. Rumours were afloat during the period of his imprisonment that he had been a party to the atrocious plots of the Thistlewood gang, and that he had escaped from the room where his coadjutors were apprehended in Cato-street, at the very moment of the entrance of the officers. This was a story, the truth of which, however, he utterly denied; but he admitted his acquaintance with a person implicated in the conspiracy who was apprehended in his presence, upon an occasion when he went to pay him a visit. We shall not go into the particulars of the whole of the tales which were circulated in reference to his past life. The public mind was so much excited during the continuance of the proceedings against him, that it would be both unfair and ungenerous to prejudice his memory by the repetition of every unproved assertion which was made. The fact which he stated of his being about to start for America on the day of his apprehension with Gale was found to be perfectly true; for it appeared that a portion of his luggage had been put on board the vessel, which, however, had sailed without its passengers on 3 April. The most remarkable part of his conduct after the dreadful murder of which he had been guilty was that which referred to a new attempt on his part to enter into the bonds of matrimony, by means of an advertisement in the public newspapers. The specious nature of his disposition is well depicted in this transaction. On 23 January, one month after the death of Mrs Brown, an advertisement appeared in the *Times* newspaper in the following terms:

> Wanted, a partner, who can command £300, to join the advertiser in a patent to bring forward a new-invented machine, of great public benefit, that is certain of realizing an ample reward. Applications by letter only (post-paid), for J.G., at Mr Bishop's, No. 1, Tudor-place, Tottenham Court-road.

The "new-invented machine" referred to in the advertisement appears to have been an apparatus for washing linen, as an article of that description was found in Greenacre's possession at the time of his being taken into custody. Among the answers to the advertisement was one from a female of great respectability, whose name and address we, for obvious reasons, abstain from making public; who, having a little money at her command, indiscreetly wrote to Greenacre on the subject, and afterwards had two or three interviews with him, without, however, coming to any arrangement. Greenacre, with that tact for which throughout the proceedings he has rendered himself so remarkable, clearly saw that it would be more advantageous to him if he could form an alliance with the lady in question, and he accordingly determined, without delay, to make her an offer of his hand, which he did in a most specious letter, written on Saturday, 4 February, the very day on which the inquest was held on the limbs of his murdered victim, and probably at the very moment while it was sitting. It was fortunate for the lady that the intimacy proceeded no farther than it did, for inevitable ruin and misery would have followed upon a matrimonial connection.

The letters to which we have alluded as having been written by Greenacre on the morning of his death were addressed to his relations and to his legal assistants, Mr Price and Mr Hobler. In both these effusions he maintained the same ground which he had taken both before and after his trial, that the death of Mrs Brown was an *accident*; and that Mrs Gale was totally unacquainted with the death of his victim until she was in custody.

Sarah Gale, it appears, had received a moderate education, and at an early period of her life is stated to have joined the theatrical corps of an East-end theatre, under the name of Wiston. From this position she sunk to that of an "unfortunate", and in that station she is stated to have been a frequent attendant at the theatres of the metropolis. While thus circumstanced she became acquainted with a member of the legal profession, with whom she lived for a considerable time, and by whom she had one child which died in its infancy. The intimacy with her protector, however, being broken off, she was considerably reduced, and was eventually married to a hackney-coachman. She now applied to the gentleman to whose acquaintance with her we have alluded, and by his assistance she was enabled to commence business in the borough of Southwark in a chandler's shop. Her husband soon dissipated all her profits; and again reduced to poverty by his desertion of her, about two years before the period of the murder, she became acquainted with Greenacre, with whom she lived at intervals up to the time of their apprehension. Her maiden name was Farr; and the child which remained with her throughout her confinement was understood to be that of her husband.

A short memoir of the life of Mrs Brown shall conclude our notice of this dreadful case. Mrs Brown, it appears, was born in the year 1780, within two miles of the city of Norwich, of respectable parents. Her maiden name was Gay. At the age of sixteen years she entered into service in the family of Lord Wodehouse, at Crimley-hall, but after remaining there for four years, she determined to come to London. For a considerable time she supported herself there as a servant, but at length she was married to a person named Thomas Brown, a shoemaker. This union proved an unhappy one, and at the expiration of two years her husband quitted her in order to proceed to Jamaica to claim some property, to which, by the death of a relation, he had become entitled. On his voyage he was washed overboard; and his wife, unacquainted with the precise nature of his claim, was unable to secure the bequest of her husband's relative. From this period she appears to have lived constantly in service, and it was supposed by her friends that she had amassed a considerable property by her savings. She was a person of reserved disposition, however, and communicated with few as to her position in life. Her acquaintance with Greenacre appears to have commenced only about three months before her murder, but the precise manner in which that connection originated does not seem to have been known to her friends.

EDITOR'S NOTE: Until a year or so ago, perhaps still, when stevedores in the London docks let fall a case of soft fruits, with the result that the case split open and the fruits rolled (the unblemished of them to be picked up and pocketed as perks), the object of the accident was referred to as "a Greenacre".

A Bedroom in Pimlico

Richard D. Altick

"THE PIMLICO MYSTERY", as the papers called it, was and was not a mystery. Everyone was pretty sure who had killed Edwin Bartlett, and to the normally cynical mind the Why was reasonably clear; but the How is unexplained to this day. As if this ambiguity were not enough to recommend it to our attention, the case is a rare blend of drama and sociological interest. From the very days when it commanded the headlines, it cried out for imaginative transferal to stage or novel, but certain of the crucial facts, without which the story would have much less meaning, could not be intelligibly dealt with except at the risk of grave offence to spectator or reader. Today, of course, there are no such taboos, and the strange history of the *ménage à trois* in a flat in Claverton Street, a story involving a tantalizing scientific puzzle, secrets of the bedchamber, and a Methodist preacher acting as a reserve husband, is available to anyone desiring to revive its unquestionable glories.

Adelaide Bartlett, a pretty, pixieish lady aged thirty, had been born at Orléans, the natural daughter of "an Englishman of good position" who was never named in the case. In 1875 her father married her to Edwin Bartlett, ten years her senior, whom, according to her story, she had seen but once before the wedding. Bartlett used her dowry to expand his holdings in a chain of six South London groceries, a business which evidently was flourishing at the time of his death. Instead of setting up a home, however, Edwin sent his twenty-year-old bride to school for two years at Stoke Newington and later, for a year, to a Belgian convent. They cohabited — using the term in its most innocent sense — only during her holidays.

It can be divined from this that Edwin Bartlett was a rather extraordinary husband. His father, a demanding, vindictive

Mrs. Adelaide Bartlett.

person who made an unfavourable impression at Adelaide's trial, testified, in all probability unaware that he was quoting Juliet's nurse's affectionate reminiscence of her late husband, that Edwin was "a very merry man". And to a certain extent this was true. Even in the last days of his life, when he was troubled by symptoms suggestive of necrosis of the jaw and mercurial poisoning, he had a robust appetite for good food. On the very eve of his death, he enjoyed half a dozen oysters at tea, jugged hare at dinner, and more oysters, as well as a chutney dish, at supper; and, figuratively rubbing his hands and licking his chops in anticipation, he desired that a large haddock be served at tomorrow's breakfast. He did not live to eat it.

But the catholicity of his sensual appetites, as we shall see, later became a matter of dispute. Along with his merriness, Edwin Bartlett entertained peculiar ideas. He believed in animal magnetism, and on one occasion, when his doctor asked him how he had slept, he answered, "I could not sleep; I was nervous and restless when I saw my wife asleep in the easy chair, so I got up and went and stood over her like this [holding up his hands] . . . for two hours, and I felt the vital force being drawn from her to me. I felt it going into me through my finger tips, and after that I laid down and slept." (Adelaide's comment: "That is a nice story. Imagine him standing for two hours and doing anything.")

Much more pertinent to the issue at hand than his exercises in reverse hypnosis, however, were his opinions respecting marriage. Witnesses testified that he believed a man should have two wives, one for companionship, the other for "use". Adelaide told Dr Leach, the aptly named physician who became desperately entangled in the fatal proceedings, that, from the outset, she and Edwin had lived by a compact of platonic marriage. This, she said, was violated on only one single, solitary occasion, at her request; and on that lone occasion she conceived a child, which, however, was born dead. Apart from this instance, they had been as continent as Adam and Eve before the Fall.

Into this queer but supposedly tranquil arrangement came, or more precisely slithered, the Reverend George Dyson, a Methodist clergyman. This pious young man immediately won the hearts of both Adelaide and her husband; soon after their acquaintance began, Edwin wrote Dyson a letter overflowing with gratitude that they had become such great friends, and a short time later he made a will leaving everything to Adelaide and appointing Dyson co-executor. When Dyson ventured to confide to Edwin scruples that occasionally afflicted him in respect to his relationship to the agreeable Adelaide, Edwin told him, in effect, not to give it a second thought. And so it was doubtless with the purest of consciences that the Reverend Mr Dyson addressed to her the following verses, a fragment of literature which in its way is surely unique in the annals of British jurisprudence.

> Who is it that hath burst the door
> Unclosed the heart that shut before
> And set her queenlike on its throne
> And made its homage all her own — My Birdie.

The Rev. George Dyson.

Perhaps this was part of Adelaide's education; for at Edwin's request, Dyson called on her almost every day to supplement her formal schooling with lessons in Latin, history, geography, and mathematics. Poetry was not specified in the curriculum, and if the above quatrain is any sign, it may well not have been included. Dyson had good educational credentials — he was B.A., Trinity College, Dublin — but it was odd that he never brought any books with him on this didactic mission, and the kind of book that was later discovered in the Claverton Street rooms was instructive only in a rather special sense.

Dyson, or "Georgius Rex" as he soon came to be known *chez* Bartlett, practically took up his daytime abode there, and when husband and wife went to Dover on holiday, he visited them at their expense. The Bartletts even bought him a season ticket from Putney, where he nominally resided, to Waterloo station, from which he could easily take a bus or even walk to Pimlico. In the flat they kept an old serge jacket and carpet slippers into which he could slip from his inhibitive clerical garb. It is not pertinent to enquire what was happening to the souls of his Wesleyan flock meanwhile.

Edwin's psyche, it may be said at this point, would have been of much interest to the young Viennese neurologist who, in the very season of Edwin's death, was enjoying his fruitful collaboration with Charcot in Paris and would, in the following autumn, return to Vienna to begin to apply his emerging principles of psychoanalysis to live patients. If Freud, as firm a believer in mesmerism as Jean Martin Charcot on the the one hand and Edwin Bartlett on the other, had exercised the art upon the latter, he might have learned much that remains obscure to us, confined as we are to the court record. Or, for that matter, nearer at home Havelock Ellis might have been professionally interested in the odd ways of this middle-aged Pimlico husband. With Edwin's enthusiastic blessing, Adelaide and Dyson indulged the pretty habit of kissing each other in his presence. Besides appointing Dyson co-executor of his will, Edwin designated their clerical friend to have reversionary rights to Adelaide after his death. Thus Dyson had the privilege of being Adelaide's fiancé even while her husband lived and relished his jugged hare. It was all very companionable. And although a servant testified that she had once entered the room to find Adelaide sitting on the floor with her head resting against the minister's knees, at no time in the trial was any allegation made that their relationship had exceeded what might be called, in a late Victorian context, the bounds of liberal propriety.

But this domestic idyll was interrupted in mid-December 1885 by Edwin's sickness. He showed signs of mercurial poisoning which were never explained, although it must be stressed that neither Adelaide nor their friend was shown to have had anything to do with it. He also had trouble with his teeth, the result of a botched job some time earlier when an incompetent dentist had sawed them off, not removed them, for the fitting of plates. He was currently in the unpleasant process of having his mouth renovated; in four visits to another dentist, eighteen badly diseased teeth were pulled. The last of these sessions occurred on the last day of the year and, as it proved, the last day of his life. In view of what happened that night, it is noteworthy that Edwin required longer than the usual dental patient to be put to sleep. He seems to have had a constitutional resistance to anaesthesia.

Notwithstanding these physical trials, however, Edwin remained a merry man. According to Dr Leach, Adelaide told him that "Edwin sits in his armchair and cries an hour at a time; and when I ask him about it, he says it was because he was so happy". It is hard, therefore, to understand why anyone should wish to upset the delicate balance of happiness with which all three were blessed at this moment. But on 28 December, Adelaide had prevailed upon Dyson to buy, at three separate chemist's shops, considerable quantities of chloroform. Edwin, she said, had been suffering for the past half-dozen years from an unspecified "internal complaint" which sometimes caused him paroxysms of pain, and it was to relieve these that chloroform was needed. Dyson, however, told the chemists, two of whom attended his chapel, that he wanted it to remove some grease spots. However reprehensible we may find a reverend clergyman's cool infraction of the biblical law against telling fibs, it is to his credit that he disdained using the old arsenic-and-rat routine.

After his return from the dentist on New Year's Eve, Edwin was in excellent spirits and, as we have seen, looked forward to a large haddock for breakfast.

Ring out the old, ring in the new. That night Adelaide, watching by his bed as usual, dropped off to sleep. A week or two earlier, upon Dr Leach's protesting that she might as well go to bed at night, since her sitting up added nothing to her husband's comfort, she had replied, "What is the use of my going to bed, Doctor? He will walk about the room like a ghost. He will not sleep unless I sit and hold his toe." "The drollness of the expression," Dr Leach commented, "fixed itself upon my mind." The drollness of the expression was matched by the drollness of the act itself; but Adelaide, who seems to have taken her husband's foibles seriously, persisted in this wifely ministration. When she awoke early New Year's morning, holding, if not his toe then at least his foot, he and it were cold. An autopsy was called for, and the chief examiner reported that the smell issuing from the stomach was that of a "freshly opened bottle of chloroform".

It was immediately after this revelation that Adelaide told Dr Leach the remarkable story of her marital existence with Edwin, some aspects of which we have already noted. She averred in addition that in the last weeks of his life, Edwin had shown unmistakable signs of reneging on their compact. But this, she said she pointed out to him, would be unfair to her as a woman as well as to her intended. To accede to one's husband's desires would constitute unfaithfulness to one's fiancé. So, to quell Edwin's ardour whenever it arose, she kept some chloroform in a drawer near their bed, to sprinkle on a handkerchief which she would then gently wave before her lustful mate's nostrils, "thinking that thereby he would go peacefully to sleep". She did not attempt to explain how the liquid chloroform entered his system from the bottle on the mantelpiece (whither it had been transferred from the drawer). Defence counsel, however, completed the story by postulating that after a chat on the subject of their renunciation of platonism, that festive New Year's Eve, Edwin, after acknowledging the justice of her views, decided to speed her and George's happiness by removing himself from the scene via the chloroform. This hypothesis had a distinct air of desperation.

Still, the prosecution too was at a disadvantage, because this was the world's first case of alleged murder by chloroform. Medical witnesses, including Dr Thomas Stevenson, who had succeeded Alfred Swaine Taylor in the chair of medical jurisprudence at Guy's Hospital and edited Taylor's standard works on the subject, agreed on cross-examination that liquid chloroform, whether taken intentionally or administered by someone else, would cause the recipient such pain as to force him to scream and would leave seared places in his mouth and throat. Yet nobody, including the landlord and his wife, who lived upstairs, had heard any sounds from the sickroom that night. The only way a murderer could hope to administer liquid chloroform without causing strenuous resistance would be to render the victim unconscious first. Yet here too was a seemingly insuperable difficulty, because unconsciousness also meant loss of the power to swallow. Dr Stevenson allowed

157

that theoretically there might be a brief interval during which "the patient might be so far insensible as not to feel the pain and yet sufficiently sensible to be able to swallow". But not even an expert could prove the existence of such a period, or when it might occur, or how long it would last. How, then, could a mere inexperienced woman succeed?

Despite the evidence against her, therefore, as the trial neared its end Adelaide probably was ahead on points. But her counsel, the great courtroom advocate Edward (later Sir Edward) Clarke, QC, MP, almost undid his case by calling back to the stand, after the prosecution's closing speech, the nurse who had attended Adelaide when she gave birth to the stillborn child. Knowing how fantastic was Adelaide's story of her non-fleshly marriage, Clarke wished to prove that it had not been concocted, for Dr Leach and thence for general distribution, *after* Edwin's death. Here was the great moment of the trial, one of the most sensationally dramatic moments in the history of English justice:

Q.　At the time you nursed Mrs Bartlett in her confinement, did you become aware from anything she said to you with regard to its having been the result of a single act?
A.　Yes, sir.

Good. The defence was eminently satisfied. But then, to Clarke's horror, Mr Justice Wills, who had often interposed peppery questions of his own during the examination of witnesses, spoke up:

Q.　What was it [that is, what the nurse had been told]?
A.　That it happened only once — on a Sunday afternoon.
Q.　She said so?
A.　Both of them; that there was always some preventive used.
Q.　You say you had that from both of them?
A.　Both of them.

So the elaborate tale of the platonic marriage was, at the very last moment, shaken; and it was toppled, during the judge's summing-up, by his recalling the testimony of a

158

policeman who had found four or five French letters (contraceptives much favoured by the Victorians) in Edwin's trousers pocket. Why, if Edwin had been as indifferent to a tumble with the ladies as he was alleged to have been, did he possess those surreptitious articles? Perhaps, of course, they had been for use outside the domestic establishment; but, as the judge said, the testimony of the nurse suggested that they might equally well have been called into requisition in connection with Adelaide. "And then," he continued as defence counsel blanched,

> what becomes of this morbid romance about the non-sexual connection, and what becomes of the man with such exalted ideas about matrimony that he thought the wife whom he elected for his companion too sacred to be touched? The whole foundation for that baseless illusion is swept away by the one sentence which you heard in the witness-box today. . . . And if the one little grain of truth which is generally to be found in any romance, in any story of falsehood, be found in these articles and in the use habitually made of them between husband and wife, what becomes of the whole story of the use for which the chloroform was wanted?

It was a compelling argument, but in the end the eloquence of Clarke's closing speech, which has been called "a classic of forensic oratory", prevailed.* The jury returned the English equivalent of Not Proven by expressing grave doubts about Adelaide's innocence but concluding that the evidence was not strong enough to convict her.

The courtroom erupted in a joyous roar. Adelaide fainted and was removed from the dock. Giving way to his emotions for the first and only time in his fifty years at the bar, Clarke dropped his head on the desk before him and sobbed. The fashionable ladies who had sat through the trial, wearing

---

* In her letter of thanks to her counsel, Adelaide wrote, "I have heard many eloquent Jesuits preach, but I never listened to anything finer than your speech." Presumably her extensive experience of Jesuit pulpit oratory was not acquired while she was in the company of the Wesleyan Mr Dyson.

Old Bailey Court—Mr. Bartlett being cross-examined by Mr. Edward Clarke, Q.C.

seasonable primroses and, according to the *Pall Mall Gazette*, drinking "deep draughts from stimulating bottles", passed from the tumult within to an even greater one outside, where their carriages waited; "their limbs", commented the reporter, who seems to have used empathy where observation failed, were "still quivering from their pleasant excitement. 'It is all over now. When shall we drink such another draught?'" When Clarke emerged into the Old Bailey courtyard, the jurymen were gathered to shake his hand in congratulations, and a cheering crowd ran alongside his brougham as it made its way through the rainy streets. The evening papers came out with great headlines, and "as one walked along from Newgate to Charing Cross, almost everyone was bending over his paper, and one heard Mrs Bartlett's name on every tongue". That night at the Lyceum Theatre, where Clarke went to see Henry Irving in *Faust*, the audience's cries were for Adelaide's triumphant lawyer, not for the actor on the stage. But it had been a near thing.

The subsequent fates of Adelaide and the Reverend Mr Dyson seem not to be known. It is at least certain that they went their separate ways; for as the judge observed in a passage of his summing-up in which he excoriated Dyson as man and as man of God, if anything was clear in this shadowy case, it was Dyson's anxiety to save his own skin. On the whole, one may doubt that he resumed his Methodist ministry. As for Adelaide, whatever became of her, she had earned a permanent niche in the history of science. Sir James Paget, the eminent surgeon, is reported to have remarked, "Once it was over, she should have told us, in the interests of science, how she did it." No Victorian murderer could have wished a finer accolade.

Nor was it only her unprecedented and inexplicable feat of killing a man with liquid chloroform that testified to Adelaide's genius for invention. There was, in addition, that bizarre narrative of the connubial arrangements in Claverton Street. But its persuasiveness did not match its audacity. Mr Justice Wills was right to call Dyson's story of Bartlett's pressing him to persevere in his intimacy with Adelaide, despite Dyson's doubts of the ethics involved, one of "almost revolting improbability"; and no less could be said for Adelaide's concomitant account. And the key that destroyed its plausibility was found in Edwin's trousers pocket. "I had a strong suspicion," the judge said, "that, before the case was over, they [the contraceptives] would throw some light upon the matter. I little anticipated what it would be. It did occur to me that this story told to Dr Leach was the poeticized version of the use of these French letters." It was difficult, he continued, after the nurse's recall to the stand and her shattering answer, "to elevate these people into the hero and heroine of an extraordinary sensational romance. It looks much more as if we had two persons to deal with, abundantly vulgar and commonplace in their habits and ways of life."

Again he was right, of course. Adelaide's confidences to Dr Leach were worthy of the queens of the sensation fiction papers, where she may have found her basic inspiration, though the embellishments probably were suggested by an imagination stimulated also by a book which played an important role in the trial. It is here that the Bartlett case contributes most signally to our knowledge of that most secretive aspect of the Victorians' private lives, about which we have only lately begun to be a little more accurately informed, namely their sexual habits. The book in question, the only book possessed by the Bartletts of which we hear anything, was *Esoteric Anthropology (The Mysteries of Man): A Comprehensive and Confidential Treatise on the Structure, Functions, Passional Attractions and Perversions, True and False Physical and Social Conditions, and the Most Intimate Relations of Men and Women,* by Thomas Low Nichols, MD, FAS, an American doctor unlicensed to practise in Britain, where he resided at the time of the trial. *Esoteric Anthropology* was one of a fair number of contemporary treatises, some with grandiose and deliberately obscure titles, some plainly and more or less honestly purporting to be works on physiology and personal hygiene, which dealt in detail or glancingly with "Malthusianism": that is, to continue the Victorian euphemism, with practices and devices which would serve as prudential checks to the production of offspring.

The history of birth control in Victorian times is very poorly documented. Because it was not a subject for open discussion, modern historians are handicapped by a paucity of dependable and relatively plain-spoken contemporary material. But it is known that, following the Malthusian campaign of the journeyman breeches-maker and radical reformer Francis Place in the 1820s, there were four decades in which little was written about birth control. The subject was resumed in the late sixties and early seventies, and in 1877 the famous case of *Regina* v. *Charles Bradlaugh and Annie Besant* gave it the most extensive publicity it had yet enjoyed. The case concerned the alleged obscenity of a work of the *Esoteric Anthropology* genre, *The Fruits of Philosophy*, by another American, Charles Knowlton, which had first been published in England, without any stir, in 1841. Thanks to the free advertising the trial afforded, 125,000 copies of this book were sold in three months, a sufficiently impressive index of the widespread public interest in birth control. Meanwhile, as testimony in the trial revealed, similar works sold steadily, year by year and without interference, in the most reputable bookshops and on railway stalls.

The sworn presence of *Esoteric Anthropology* and contraceptives in the Bartletts' rooms is a valuable, because rare, fragment of historical evidence. It suggests how extensively the knowledge and practice of birth control had been disseminated by the mid-eighties, and it supplies a documented example of one reason why the birth rate among the middle class declined in the latter half of the Victorian era. No historian of late Victorian morals and mores nor any student of population trends has, I think, used this trial to illustrate the prevalance of contraceptive information and practice at the time.

And although Adelaide was herself no bluestocking and no feminist, in her sexual role, if we read it aright, she may be regarded as an immediate precursor of the "New Woman" of the nineties, who claimed the right to free love and evasion of motherhood. The intimate policy and practices in Claverton Street obviously were the result of Edwin's idiosyncrasy rather than ideology, but it is interesting to note that the Bartletts' marital arrangements came into public view at the very time that the women's emancipation movement was gathering momentum. Two influential papers setting forth advanced ideas on women's rights, *The Woman Question* and *Socialism and Sex*, by the socialist university lecturer and eugenicist Karl Pearson, appeared, respectively, in the year preceding the trial and the year following it. Whether or not Adelaide and Edwin were even aware of the currents of advanced thought in respect to love and marriage in the late 1880s — and nothing adduced at the trial suggested they were — their rejection of the strict ideal of monogamy in favour of a permissiveness governed by spontaneous emotional preference and their use of contraceptives in preference to the Malthusian "prudential continence" had the accidental effect of identifying them with the avant garde. Thus, in its own special way, the Bartlett case is closely linked to a particular moment in history.

Judge Wills, however, saw nothing of potential historical value in the revelations from the witness box. He was lengthily caustic about books like *Esoteric Anthropology* — "garbage" which "under the garb of ostentatious purity, obtains entrance, probably, into many a household from which it would be otherwise certain to be banished". It was undoubtedly the perusal of its evilly instructive and stimulating pages that "unsexed" countless women, who thereby were rendered willing, nay eager, to hear the minutest details of the sordid case now nearing completion; and in the special instance of Adelaide Bartlett, he said, "one has learnt today what is the natural and to be expected consequences of indulgence in literature of that kind".

Perhaps so, perhaps not. Adelaide's reading alone cannot account for her inventiveness. She was a magnificent natural improviser, and it is impossible not to believe that talents like hers were squandered both on the technique with which she disposed of her odd husband and on the extravagant coloration she gave to her purported relations with him. Her genius deserved a loftier arena, a wider scope.

Similarly, one feels that Mr Justice Wills's moralizing was not worthy of the case or of the judge himself, who deserves a special word before we take leave of him and the fair Adelaide of whom he so obviously disapproved. Of all the judges who presided over famous Victorian trials, he is among the most interesting — and the most complex. We have noted how his worldly wisdom, his cynical shrewdness, enabled him to see through the bogus romanticism of Adelaide's version of her love life with Edwin and to deduce the significance of the French letters. He seems to have laboured under few illusions as to the moral strength, not to say the probity, of his fellow men. The evidence of their weakness in the Bartlett case saddened him but did not surprise him, and we sense that his denunciation of printed "garbage" was more or less *pro forma*, the sort of thing any Victorian judge would have felt obliged to say. Yet it was this same judge who, ten years later, charging the jury in the Oscar Wilde–Alfred Taylor trial, declared, "I would rather try the most shocking murder case that it has ever fallen to my lot to try than be engaged in a case of this description," and who, addressing the defendants after the jury had found them guilty, said: "It is no use for me to address you. People who can do these things must be dead to all sense of shame, and one cannot hope to produce any effect upon them. This is the worst case I have ever tried. . . . That you, Wilde, have been the centre of a circle of the most hideous kind among young men, it is equally impossible to doubt." In contrast to the cheers of approval after Adelaide Bartlett was acquitted, Mr Justice Wills's sentence of Wilde to two years at hard labour drew cries of "Oh! Oh!" and "Shame!"

No contradiction is necessarily involved, of course. The moral indignation evoked by each of the two cases was of very different quality. At the turn of the century, sodomy was a virtually unspeakable offence, while murder, with or without adultery, was at least a fairly commonplace and comprehensible transaction. Moreover, Wills, as the record of his interventions and charge to the jury in the Bartlett trial makes clear, had a divided nature. One side of him was experienced, unflappable; the other side was puritanical, morally intolerant, in the gravest Victorian tradition. His role in the Bartlett case is a study in contrasts.

His moralizing, *in re* Bartlett no less than *in re* Wilde, has not worn well. But no one could possibly fault one dictum of his, in the course of his summing-up, which is as sage in the ways of the world as it was on the day it was uttered from the bench in the Old Bailey: "When a young wife and a younger male friend get to discussing, whether in the presence of the husband or out of his presence, the probability of his decease within a measurable time, and the possibility of the friend succeeding to that husband's place, according to all ordinary experience of human life that husband's life is not one that an insurance office would like to take at any premium."

The Slaying of Léon Beron

H.M. Walbrook

ONE DOES NOT connect Clapham Common with the battle, murder, and sudden death from which we pray in the Litany to be delivered. Thither long ago journeyed the charming John Evelyn to visit his friend, Mr Pepys, in his "very noble and wonderfully well furnished house and garden well accommodated for pleasure and retirement". There, in a later age, walked the younger Pitt with William Wilberforce and Thomas Clarkson, discussing together the betterment of mankind. There, in the latter days of Queen Victoria, a young Socialistic engineer named John Burns, who lived to be the first Labour member of a British Cabinet, was wont to air his florid oratory under the Red Flag. And there today flourish cricket in the summer, football in the winter, and every sort of Sunday afternoon platform propaganda all the year round.

On New Year's Day, 1911, however, this breezy South London upland received another and far uglier advertisement. Early on that morning the corpse of a man was discovered lying among some thorn bushes and fallen leaves by the side of an asphalt path leading from the bandstand towards Battersea Rise. He had obviously been murdered, apparently between the hours of 2 a.m. and 3 a.m., and the marks on the body showed that his assailant had displayed not only a brutality but also a caprice in his methods, suggesting that his motive had been something different from the mere anger or cupidity usual in such cases. The corpse showed the wounds of eight heavy blows on the head, four deep stabs in the stomach, and, on the face, a long, curious cut on each cheek, made in the shape of the "f" opening on either side of the bridge of a violin. These disfigurements had evidently been inflicted after death, and the police called them "S" cuts, for the reason that they also bore a similarity to the form of that letter. When the dead man was identified as one Léon Beron, a Russian Jew of French extraction who had been living in Whitechapel, it was at once concluded in the newspapers that the "S" thus carved on the face stood for "Spy", and that the crime had been one of political vengeance.

Whitechapel at that time was seething with foreign anarchism. Not long before, an alien living in that neighbourhood had leapt from an omnibus with a revolver, firing at everybody at random, and killing people. In the very week of the murder on Clapham Common, the so-called "Battle of Sidney Street" took place, in which a nest of foreign anarchists (associated with a notorious individual known as "Peter the Painter") defied the police in a house in that thoroughfare, and had to be suppressed by the fire of soldiery. In short, all the evil reports which the crimes of "Jack the Ripper" had shed upon the district more than twenty years before were, in those early days of 1911, wrapping it in a still blacker cloud. The whole foreign community of Whitechapel had come to be regarded as a kind of cancer in the English body politic.

Hence the excitement over the Clapham Common tragedy. Who had brought Léon Beron right across London at such an hour to slay him with such violence, and then with brutal fantasy to carve those emblems on his cheeks? Obviously, declared the evening newspapers, Nihilism was at the back of it. Presently, however, another and more commonplace theory began to be ventilated. Inquiries in Whitechapel elicited the fact that the dead man had been regarded among his acquaintances as a man of property and "an independent gentleman". In other words, he had been in the habit of carrying from ten to thirty pounds of gold and notes in his pockets. He had also been the possessor of a heavy gold watch attached to a massive gold chain, from the other end of which hung a five-pound gold piece. When the corpse was searched by the police, the watch and chain had disappeared, and the only money found in the pockets was a halfpenny.

Exactly a week later, an arrest was made. On the morning of 8 January, a young Russian Jew, well known in the neighbourhood of Whitechapel, and living in Newark Street

under the name of Steinie Morrison, while breakfasting in a cheap restaurant in Fieldgate Street, off the Whitechapel Road, was suddenly surrounded by five police officers and conveyed to the police-station in Leman Street. The reason for such a number taking part in the arrest was the fact that Morrison was already known to the police, that he was a man of formidable physique, and that he was believed to be carrying a loaded revolver about with him. Two five-pound notes were found on him, together with four pounds in gold and other money; and, although the word was not mentioned by his captors, he seemed at once to realize that the charge against him was one of murder.

He had lately been earning a living by such varied means as bread-making, peddling small jewellery, stealing and burglary. Among his numerous pseudonyms were Moses Tagger and Morris Tagger. His real name appears to have been Alexander Petropavloff. An important link in the story now brought against him by the police was the fact that the bakery in which he had been employed in the preceding September,

168

Morrison in the dock

October, and November was on Lavender Hill, close to a turning leading directly to the very spot on Clapham Common at which Beron's mutilated corpse had been discovered.

Later in the day, he was brought up at the South London Police-court on Lavender Hill to answer the charge. The evening papers had given the usual publicity to the morning's arrest, and the court was so crowded with reporters and photographers that even the space round the dock swarmed with them — "to the great disgust", said a spectator, "of the unemployed and other regular attendants at the back of the court." They had all heard of the crime, with its mixture of brutality and strangeness. They had also read that the arrested man was a Russian Jew from Whitechapel — and it is not difficult to guess the sort of person they expected to see enter the dock. Presumably a figure like the Mr Hyde in Robert Louis Stevenson's story of the criminal haunting the purlieus of Soho — something pale, dwarfish, and deformed, a creature inspiring disgust, loathing, and fear. What was their surprise when a tall, clean-shaven, handsome and well-dressed young man, with a high, broad forehead, well-recessed dark eyes, and pleasingly arched eyebrows stepped briskly forward, and stood very erect confronting the magistrate and the crowded court! There was nothing harsh or forbidding in his face. His manner was soft and gentle. As he stood there calmly listening to what was being said against him, he might, said an onlooker, have been a reticent philanthropist. He seemed to have no idea whatever that he was in any sort of peril.

The police-court inquiry proved to be a prolonged one. It had to be adjourned more than once; and now and then the accused man's composure broke down. On one occasion a young Whitechapel Jewess, a girl of the streets, swore that on the afternoon of the murder he had visited her, wearing on his watch-guard a five-pound gold piece similar to one which she had formerly seen hanging from the dead man's chain. At that, he burst forth with a voice that rang through the court: "Do you know you are telling lies, eh? You are taking my life away from me! Do think well what you are saying! Before God it isn't truth she is saying! She is telling lies! Lies! She never saw me with the five-pound piece! Never at all! She is telling lies!" On the following day the girl confessed that she had been mistaken.

Again, when it was stated that Morrison was a left-handed man and that blood-stains had been discovered on the left side of his clothes, he lost his temper and shouted at the top of his voice: "That's a lie!" And once more, as between the witness and the accused, the latter seemed the more credible.

There were also moments of sentimentality and even of humour in the proceedings. One individual, describing the esteem in which the accused was held by his neighbours in Newark Street, said: "He went out every evening dressed in a different suit: he was quite a gentleman!" — a sentence which recalled Carlyle's famous "gigmanity" in the Thurtell case.

The baker who had employed him at his establishment on Lavender Hill said of him: "He was a smart, intelligent fellow, most gentlemanly, very fond of children, playful and affectionate with them; apparently a teetotaller, punctual at his work, and first-rate with the fancy bread."

The evidence incriminating him, however, was felt to outweigh these tributes, and in the end he was committed to take his trial on the capital charge at the Central Criminal Court. He listened to the decision with outward composure, and on his way back to Brixton Gaol amazed the officer in charge by asking if he could oblige him with a cigar. While he was in prison awaiting his trial, all sorts of shady aliens, male and female, young and old, called with the tenderest enquiries.

The trial opened on the following 6 March before Mr Justice Darling, with Mr Richard Muir as leading Counsel for the Crown and Mr Edward Abinger as leading Counsel for the defence.

The case for the prosecution was unfolded as follows: For a fortnight or so before the murder, Beron (a short, stoutish man of forty-eight) and the prisoner had often been seen together at a popular foreign eating-house in Osborn Street, Whitechapel, called the Warsaw, but chiefly known as Snelwar's restaurant, and the younger man had visibly struck up a considerable friendship with him. Late on the night of 31 December 1910, the pair left the restaurant together, Beron apparently slightly the worse for drink, and Morrison having in his possession a bar of iron wrapped in brown paper. At two o'clock in the morning, they drove together in a cab from Whitechapel to a point opposite the Shakespeare Theatre on Lavender Hill, where they got out. Morrison paid the cabman his fare, five shillings, and the vehicle drove away. At a quarter past three on the same morning, Morrison, now unaccompanied, hailed another cab at the eastern end of Clapham Common, and was driven to Kennington, where he got out and walked towards Kennington Gate. There he met a man with whom he entered into conversation. He presently called a taxi, and drove with

Léon Beron

his new companion to the north side of the river, alighting at Finsbury Park. He had apparently disposed of the dead man's watch and chain to the individual who met him at Kennington. Later that morning he deposited a revolver and a box of cartridges in the cloakroom at St Mary's Station, Whitechapel, giving his name as "Banman". That afternoon he made the acquaintance of a young woman living in York Road, Lambeth, and made arrangements to live with her. After that he was arrested.

For the defence, the story was that early on the evening of 31 December he went to Snelwar's restaurant and had a substantial tea; that the brown-paper parcel he was carrying, and which had been said to contain an iron bar, contained nothing more harmful than a flute; that after he had finished his meal he asked the waiter to take charge of the parcel, and walked off to the Shoreditch Empire of Varieties for the "second show", beginning at nine o'clock. After the performance, he returned to the restaurant, had a glass of lemonade, received his flute back from the waiter, left a few minutes before midnight, unaccompanied, walked to his rooms in Newark Street, passing Léon Beron on the way in the company of a tall stranger, responded to Beron's customary "Bonsoir, Monsieur," let himself in with his latchkey, went to bed, and did not get up again until between nine and ten o'clock on the following morning, when he dressed, went to the neighbouring baths, and generally resumed his ordinary way of living.

For nine days the trial went on, and seldom can a judge or jury have had to listen to so extraordinary a contrast of witnesses — English physicians, police officers, clerks and cabmen alternating with the flotsam and jetsam of the Ghetto in the form of loafers, receivers of stolen goods, pimps, panders, harlots and brothelkeepers.

Half of these foreigners knew no other language than Yiddish, and had to speak through an interpreter, and several of them could neither read nor write. A furrier, said to be of German origin, swore that he had seen Morrison and Beron together a couple of times at the Warsaw restaurant, and, on being asked by counsel what he meant by "a couple of times", replied "It can be ten times; it can be more." A young waiter, a native of Galicia, was unable to name the month or the day of the month on which he was giving evidence. One gift and one only they all seemed to share to perfection — that of telling falsehoods. Seldom can even the walls of the Old Bailey have listened to such a spate of glib and shameless lying as these aliens emitted. It was the old story of the gulf that lies between the Oriental and the Western way of handling facts.

Consequently Mr Abinger, who in his long career at the Bar had defended many a prisoner and restored him, as the song in the opera goes, "to his friends and his relations", now found himself up against a wall of prejudice formidable indeed. As a result he now and then said things that were the reverse of tactful. He allowed himself to be humorous at the expense of the judge. In the course of a discussion over one of the witnesses for the prosecution who had emitted a particularly glaring falsehood, Mr Justice Darling let fall the observation that he had been musing upon a certain remark of the Royal Psalmist, "I said in my haste all men are liars." "Gentlemen," responded Mr Abinger, turning to the jury, "I wish I had the remarkable abilities of my Lord, who is able to allow his mind the luxury of dwelling upon King David while we are discussing this sordid case. Gentlemen, of course you know his Lordship's literary talents. I have none." It was rather a laborious piece of irony at the best. Worse than that, it was deplorably out of place. Into another of his tiffs he introduced a phrase which can scarcely have caused much elation in the jury-box. The judge had given him a certain warning on a point of law, and, in an obviously quick-tempered reply, Mr Abinger allowed himself to say, "It does not require the intellect *even of this jury* to understand what your Lordship means."

As it happened, the warning in question had been a highly important one. In a discursive cross-examination of two of the witnesses for the prosecution, Mr Abinger, by means of questions entirely unconnected with the issue before the court, had proved them to be persons of doubtful character. Mr Justice Darling's warning was that, as a result of that procedure, the prosecution had the power under the Criminal Evidence Act, 1898, to cross-examine the prisoner on the whole of his past record — a course which Mr Muir duly proceeded to adopt, with devastating results. In a deadly pelting of questions he forced Morrison to entangle himself in contradiction after contradiction, to admit that he had been in prison for stealing, that he had served sentences of six months, fifteen months and five years for burglary or offences connected with burglary, and that in an effort made in prison to secure his deportation from England, he had written a letter to the Home Secretary containing a number of palpable falsehoods. In short, he made him confess to the court that during practically the whole of his eleven or twelve years in England, he had been living the life of a criminal.

Throughout this prolonged ordeal, the accused man, whether as a display of irony or of innocence, maintained an extraordinary composure. He smilingly derided the story of the "bar of iron wrapped in brown paper". Even in his labours as a housebreaker, he pleasantly asked, of what use would a bar of iron have been? He had his carpenter's chisel. That was enough. "And what do you use a chisel for?" asked Mr Muir. "To get into the house," came the calm reply. "To get in through a window without waking the inhabitants?" suggested counsel. "Exactly. To get in through a window without waking the inhabitants," echoed the prisoner, significantly adding, "As a rule, the places I commit burglaries in are gentlemen's houses in which the inhabitants sleep upstairs, and there is nobody down below. In the East End you couldn't get in and out of a window by night. There there are people living in every room."

Once and once only did he display passion. A good-looking young Jewess, sixteen years of age, Jane Brodsky by name, had appeared as one of the witnesses for the defence, and Morrison had been described as having wished to marry her. In the course of his cross-examination, Mr Muir asked him if he had ever taken her for an infamous purpose to a house of ill fame. "Never!" he cried, his eyes flashing as he spoke. "Jane Brodsky is as pure and innocent a girl as there ever was in the world! She is as pure and innocent a girl as anybody's daughter, and anybody saying anything against that is a liar!"

Mr Abinger's final speech on the prisoner's behalf was interrupted by another extraordinary exhibition of the Jewish temperament. Earlier in the proceedings, an elder brother of the dead man, Solomon Beron, had given a quantity of rambling evidence, in the course of which he described himself as, among other things, an independent gentleman living at Rowton House, and paying sixpence or sevenpence a night for his bed. At a moment when Mr Abinger was at the height of his earnestness, this brother, whose mind had visibly been unhinged by the tragedy, suddenly sprang from his place, rushed at him, caught hold of him and screamed, "Stop! Stop! You are trying to save a murderer! The murderer of my brother!" A number of police officers seized him. "Go away! Go away!" he shrieked. "He is trying to get that man off!" Eventually he was lifted out of the court, carried to the outer entrance and deposited on the pavement, still yelling, "Go away!" and "Murder!" to the amazement of the crowd in the street. He was not permitted to enter the court again.

In his long and able charge to the jury, Mr Justice Darling made no secret of the anxiety the whole case had caused him. He clearly suggested that the murder had possibly been the work not of one man but of two, one of them inflicting the blows on the head with the alleged bar of iron, and the other inflicting the stabs with the knife. As to the so-called "S" cuts of which so much had been made, he dismissed them with the words, "Anyone who sees the letter 'S' in either of these scratches has either better eyes or a more vivid imagination than I can claim to possess." In a solemn passage he warned the jury against allowing themselves to be prejudiced by the account of the prisoner's criminal career which had been extracted from him in the witness-box. He also pointed out the danger of accepting "identifications" of an accused person which had been preceded by seeing photographs of him in the newspapers, and forcibly described the Press publication of such photographs as a practice calculated to frustrate the ends of justice. Viewing the whole case, he reminded them that the prisoner "may be guilty and yet may not be *proved* to be guilty", and told them with the utmost gravity that they were bound to give him the benefit of any doubt.

The gentlemen in the jury-box, however, had seemingly already made up their minds. They were only thirty-five minutes considering their verdict, and on their return into court they declared through their foreman that they had found the prisoner "Guilty". A couple of minutes sufficed for what followed. The judge did not, as generally happens, express his concurrence with the verdict. In addressing the prisoner, all he said was, "The jury have arrived at the only conclusion as it appears to them consistent with the whole of the evidence against you," adding that the only duty left him was that of passing the judgment awarded by the law. When the sentence's concluding words, "and may the Lord have mercy on your soul", had died away, Steinie Morrison allowed himself one last outburst. "I decline such mercy!" he cried. "Neither do I believe that there is a God in Heaven!" With that he turned, and, with head haughtily erect, passed out of sight.

As it happened, he was destined after all to die in his bed. The Court of Criminal Appeal upheld his conviction, but a petition on his behalf to the Home Secretary of the day (Mr Winston Churchill) led to a reprieve from the supreme authority in the land, King George V. While making no reflection on the reasonableness of the jury's verdict, Mr Churchill, in advising His Majesty, implied that much in the case had been unexplained, leaving room for a doubt that might perhaps be cleared up later, and of which the prisoner was entitled to the benefit. As usual, the substitution of the gaol for the scaffold evoked a quantity of criticism, and the customary cry was heard again in full force: "If the man is proved guilty he should be hanged. If he is not proved guilty he should be acquitted." It is an ancient fallacy. It is the familiar difference between being apparently guilty in fact and yet not apparently guilty in law.

No impartial student of the report of the case in the *Notable British Trials* series can doubt that, in the face of such a mass of incriminating statements, the jury's verdict was inevitable. It is impossible to resist the theory that the young Whitechapel burglar who had known Léon Beron as a person with money and valuables on him, and who was intimately familiar with Lavender Hill and Clapham Common, was the man who led him in the dark of that New Year's morning to the place where his dead body was afterwards found. Morrison tried in the witness-box to make out that at the time of the murder he was in possession of ample means, yet the fact was established that he had been reduced to pawning his watch-chain only a week before. It was also proved that Beron was under the influence of drink when he left Snelwar's restaurant at midnight of 31

December. Obviously, to kill and rob such a man in a remote place and in the loneliest and the safest hour of the night was a far easier and likely to be a far more profitable job than breaking into a gentleman's house with the aid of a chisel. There may, as the judge hinted, have been two men in the murder. Obviously, if there were, Morrison could not dare to admit it; and in the years which have elapsed since the tragedy, no *particeps criminis* has been identified.

It only remains to be said that Morrison lived ten years longer, and that during his incarceration all the ferocity of temperament with which he had been charged at the Old Bailey manifested itself only too plainly. He incurred repeated punishments for savage assaults upon his warders, and begged again and again to be hanged and put out of his misery. In the end, he practically committed suicide by refusing his food, and died on 24 January 1921, in the prison infirmary. To the last he declared himself innocent of the death of Léon Beron; but few who knew him in Dartmoor or Parkhurst doubted that if he had contrived to secure possession of a bar of iron or a long knife, and the chance had offered, he would have killed a warder.

Murder of a Minder

Anonymous

AN ATROCIOUS MURDER was committed on the night of Monday, 1 January 1828, upon the body of a woman seventy-five years old, named Elizabeth Jeffe, who had the care of an unoccupied house belonging to a respectable gentleman named Lett, and situated at No. 11, Montague-place, Russell-square.

It appears that Mr Lett resided at Dulwich, and the house in Montague-place, which he had formerly occupied, being to let, he had placed the unfortunate Mrs Jeffe in it to take care of it, and to exhibit its rooms to any person who might be desirous of renting it.

On the evening of Monday, 1 January, she was last seen alive by Gardner, the pot-boy of the Gower Arms public-house, Gower-street, who delivered a pint of beer to her, and then she was in conversation at the door with a young man, dressed in a blue coat, and wearing a white apron.

On the following day the house remained closed, contrary to custom, and some suspicion being entertained that something serious had occurred to cause this unusual circumstance, information was conveyed to Mr Justice Holroyd, who resided in the same street, whose butler, with the porter of Mr Robinson, an upholsterer, proceeded to the house. Some difficulty was at first experienced in obtaining admittance; but the back area door having been forced, the unfortunate woman was found lying in a front room on the basement story, with her throat dreadfully cut and quite dead.

Mr Plum, a surgeon of Great Russell-street, was immediately sent for, and on his arrival, he proceeded to an examination of the person of the deceased. He found that she had been dead during several hours, and that her death had obviously been caused by the loss of blood occasioned by the

179

wound in her throat, which extended through the windpipe and gullet, and the large vessels on the right side of the neck. The handkerchief of the deceased had been thrust into the wound, but from the appearances which presented themselves, it became obvious that the foot and not the hand had been employed to place it in the position in which it was found. On the left collar-bone there were some bruises, as if produced by some person's knuckles, and upon the thighs there were similar marks, as well as some drops of blood, but no wound was discovered besides that in the throat, to which death could be attributable.

Upon a further inspection of the deceased's clothes, it was discovered that her pockets had been rifled; but although the kitchen drawers were open, and bore the bloody impress of fingers, and a work-basket was similarly stained, there was nothing further to show that the object of the murderer, which was evidently plunder, had been attained. The neck-handkerchief and cap-ribbon of the wretched woman were cut through, apparently in the effort to inflict the wound; and independently of the opinion of Mr Plum, that the deceased could not have cut herself to such an extent, the fact of her death being caused by the hand of another was clearly shown by the absence of any instrument with which the wound could have been inflicted, although part of a razor-case was found lying on the floor.

Upon an examination of the house being made, it was found that the hall door was merely on the latch, and the furniture in the parlour presented an appearance which showed that the murderer had gone into that apartment after the death of his victim. A publication headed "The State of the Nation" was found there smeared with blood, and a doe-skin glove for the right hand, on which marks of blood were also visible, was discovered lying on the floor.

From circumstances which came to light, the officers who were employed to endeavour to trace out the perpetrators of this atrocious murder were induced to suspect that Charles Knight, the son of the deceased, was in some measure implicated in its commission. By direction of Mr Halls, the magistrate of Bow-street, who throughout the whole case exhibited the most unremitting desire to secure the ends of justice, he was apprehended at his lodgings in Cursitor-street; but upon his being questioned, he gave a clear and unembarrassed statement of the manner in which he had been engaged during the night of the murder, and inquiry having proved this to be true, he was ordered to be discharged.

The police were now completely at a loss to fix upon any person as being open to suspicion. The man who had been seen in conversation with the deceased at the door of her house, however, appeared to be pointed at by common consent, and an accident soon pointed out a person named William Jones as the individual suspected. It was learned that he had been in the habit of calling upon the deceased at her master's residence, and that he was a seafaring man; but beyond these circumstances, and that he had been living in Mitre-street, Lambeth, nothing could be learned of him or his pursuits.

On inquiry being made at his lodgings, it was discovered that he had absconded, and the suspicion of his guilt, which was already entertained, was greatly strengthened by this circumstance. A reward of £10 was offered for his apprehension, and by a remarkable accident on Monday, 13 January he was taken into custody by a city officer, on a charge of stealing a coat. He was then taken to Guildhall office, but Salmon, the Bow-street officer, having claimed him on this charge, he was delivered over to his custody, and by him conveyed to Bow-street. He there most strenuously denied that he was at all implicated in the murder, although he admitted that "he had done other things," but he was remanded for the production of further evidence.

From subsequent inquiries, it was learned that he was the son of Mr Stephen Jones, a gentleman well known in the literary world as the author of a dictionary called *Jones' Sheridan Improved*, and as the editor of a journal published in London. This gentleman, who died only a short time before the Christmas preceding the murder, left two sons, who possessed considerable talents, but who were too much inclined to habits of dissipation. William Jones had gone to sea, but latterly, on his return, being so much straitened in his circumstances as to be sometimes in actual want, he had occasionally visited Mrs Jeffe, who was a kind-hearted woman, and who, from the respect which she bore his family, had often relieved his necessities. At the time of his apprehension he was twenty-five years of age, and was dressed in a blue coat, as described by Gardner, the pot-boy, by whom he was seen talking to the deceased.

Upon his subsequent examinations, the material facts which were proved against him were, that he had been living with a young woman, named Mary Parker, who generally went by the name of Edwards, in Wootton-street, Lambeth; but that on 27 December, he suddenly removed with her to Mitre-street. During the latter part of his residence in Wootton-street, he was in extremely bad circumstances, and on 31 December, he and his paramour were entirely without food or money.

On that night he quitted Parker in Fleet-street, and appointed to meet her at the same place at half-past twelve o'clock, and at that hour he came to her, as she was standing near Serjeants' Inn, in a direction from Shoe-lane. He then had money and treated her to something to drink; and on the following morning he went out for an hour, but returned, and now produced a considerable quantity of silver money, with which they were enabled to redeem some clothes, which had been pawned, and afterwards to go to the Olympic Theatre. In the course of the ensuing week, the prisoner was observed to be anxiously endeavouring to prevent the discovery of his new residence, by going home by circuitous routes, and other means, and was heard to declare his apprehension that some officers were in search of him; but the most important circumstances proved were, first, that of the prisoner having a severe cut on his left thumb, when he was taken into custody, which appeared to have been recently inflicted; and secondly, that the razor-case, which was found lying near the body of the deceased woman, had been lent to the prisoner, on the Sunday before the murder, with a razor, by Mrs Williams, with whom he had formerly lodged. Upon proof of these facts, the prisoner was fully committed for trial; but strong as the suspicion was against him, it proved to be insufficient in the minds of the jury, before whom the case was tried, to warrant them in returning a verdict of guilty.

The case came on at the Old Bailey sessions, on Friday, 22 February, when considerable curiosity was exhibited by the public. The court was crowded to excess at an early hour, and its avenues were thronged until the conclusion of the proceedings. The prisoner was put to the bar at ten o'clock, and pleaded Not Guilty to the two indictments preferred against him; the first for the murder, and the second for stealing a coat, the property of George Holding. Having been given in charge to the jury in the first case, the evidence which we have given in substance was detailed by the various witnesses. The prisoner on being called on for his defence read a paper, in which he complained of the prejudices which had been excited against him, and solemnly asserted his innocence of the crime imputed to him. He entered into a long argumentative statement, contending that no grounds what-ever existed for believing him guilty of the murder; and witnesses having been called on his behalf, who swore that his disposition was both mild and humane, the trial terminated at twelve o'clock at night, when the jury returned a verdict of Not Guilty.

The prisoner was arraigned on the next day upon the second indictment, when he withdrew the plea which he had put on the record, and confessed himself guilty. At the following sessions, held in the month of April, he was sentenced to be transported for seven years; in pursuance of which, he was sent to Van Diemen's Land. Some surprise was excited at his having escaped thus easily from the hands of justice, as it was known that there were charges of forgery to a considerable extent pending against him; and it was suggested that some persons of respectability and good standing had interested themselves in his behalf.

It has been reported that he has been executed in Hobart Town, for bush-ranging, and that before his death he confessed himself guilty of the murder for which he was tried;

but although the idea gained currency at the time of its being thrown out, we have no means of ascertaining the degree of credit to which the story is entitled.

Sam's New-Year Resolution

Jonathan Goodman

THE SCENE OF THE KILLING and furnacing of Walter Spatchett was one of two rooms in a shack that served as the office and stores of a building firm at 30 Hawley Crescent, in the North London district of Camden Town, less than a mile south-west of the house where, twenty-three years before, in January 1910, Dr Hawley Crippen killed and fragmented the remains of Belle Elmore. The two cases — one almost forgotten, the other still renowned — have more in common than the propinquity of their beginnings. Each involved the police in what the newspapers of the respective times blared as "HISTORY'S GREATEST MAN-HUNT"; both made footnotes to the history of wireless.

At the start of 1933, the building firm, S.J. Furnace & Co., had been in existence, but only just, for eighteen months. Samuel James Furnace employed three men and a boy. Most of his own time was spent touting for business. Since setting up the firm, he had rarely been left with much of a profit at the end of a week of grafting after paying wages (which, even if it meant borrowing, he had done without fail), dealing with final demands for the rent of the yard and for payment for materials supplied on credit terms, and (most important to him, this, for he doted upon his wife May and their three small children) covering his family's living expenses and —aided by rent from a lodger, an old friend named William Abbott — keeping up the mortgage on their home, a terrace house in Crogsland Road, off Haverstock Hill, a few minutes' walk from Hawley Crescent. So far as anyone in Camden Town seems to have been aware, Furnace, a teetotaller and non-smoker, needed only small change for pocket-money: sufficient for him to stand his rounds of cups of tea or coffee with acquaintances in a café near the Underground station, to pay his half of table hire-charges in a billiards saloon in Delancey Street, close to the Bedford Music Hall.

He was forty-two years of age, a native of the peaceful shire of Huntingdon. I shall not try to describe him, because, as will appear, he was protean in snap-shots. He had no formal qualifications as a decorator, let alone as a builder. Prior to the Great War, and for some time from two or three years after the Armistice, he had been a ship's steward; he had served in the army during the war, and had then spent a couple of years in the south of Ireland as an auxiliary policeman — a Black and Tan. Perhaps it was Sinn-Feiners who had left him with the scars of gunshot wounds on both arms and on his left leg, and with a long scar, showing the marks of thirteen stitches, on his right bicep. Perhaps a loaded Webley revolver that he kept in a drawer of his desk in the smaller of the two rooms in his business shack was a souvenir — an illicit one: he did not have a firearms certificate — of his service in what was now called Eire.

Those ballistical uncertainties concerning Furnace could probably have been cleared up by a man who was quoted anonymously on the front page of the *News of the World* of 15 January 1933:

> Furnace and I were together in Ireland in 1921, he in the Black and Tans and I in the regular R[oyal] I[rish] C[onstabulary]. After I left Ireland I saw nothing more of him till July of last year. Then I bumped into him accidentally in Aldwych. In the meantime I myself had been in serious trouble in London — so serious that it came to a prosecution. Furnace had read all about the case and my acquittal, and congratulated me on the result. He seemed happy enough then.
>
> Ten weeks ago I met him again, this time at the bus stop outside Chalk Farm Station [near Crogsland Road]. We turned into a café and talked of the old days for an hour. After that, we discussed various disappearance mysteries, aliases that had been used, and alibis.
>
> He knew that at the peril of my life I had once been back to Ireland after the Troubles, and wanted to know how it was done. I explained that in Glasgow I embarked on a ship at the Broomielaw for Belfast, and then entrained for Dublin. I was searched at

Dundalk, on the border, found in possession of a revolver, and sent back home.

"Do they search you at the border now?" Furnace asked, and I told him that, so far as I was aware, they examined only baggage, and not the person. After that, he wanted to know the rates of pay in the Free State and the Republican armies, and when I laughed at the prospect of him enlisting in either he stopped me and said, "Don't laugh, but look at this." He produced his old discharge papers, and, pointing to the name, explained how easily the "J" (representing James) could be converted into an "O", an apostrophe added, and the same changed to Samuel O'Furnace.

"But they would soon tumble who you were," I reminded him, "and don't forget, Sam, you were once in the Black and Tans."

"Yes, that's just it," he agreed. "Well, there's another way. Supposing a man could get to Dublin, it would be easy to tramp to the west side and hide up in Mayo or Connemara. None of the natives has learned to read up there, and if anyone went after him from England, they would hinder them rather than help."

I told him I did not agree.

"Well, you don't know the West of Ireland," he said. "When I was there, hundreds of police searched for months for three men up and down the West Coast, and couldn't get them. And at no time were the three men a mile from Croughpatrick mountain. So that's where I might be going one day — to Mayo or Connemara."

Just one other thing. Before I left him on that afternoon ten weeks ago, he said, "Look here, ——, supposing a fellow couldn't get to Ireland. What about Canada or America? How would he manage that?"

I told him of an experience of my own. Scores of men come over from the States and Canada each month on the cattle-boats to Liverpool. They always possess a return ticket by the same line, and in the company's books are rough descriptions of each cattleman. Lots of these men prefer to stay in England. They can be found every day in a well-known hostelry near the Liverpool docks, and hang on to their return tickets until some potential purchaser comes along prepared to pay a pound or so for a cheap passage across the Atlantic. All this I told Furnace. He thought for a moment. Then he said, "Let's see. What's the name of that pub where these fellows hang out?"

Carefully he wrote the address in a note-book. "I must remember that," he said. . . .

Round about Christmas, 1932 — some three months after Furnace's quizzing of his former comrade-in-arms — he made a special trip to the local office of the Britannic Assurance Co., there to hand to the manager, Mr Macdonald Smith, the sum of £28 16s. 6d, that being the second annual premium on a policy insuring his life for £1,000 — plus £100 a year till 1951, should his death occur in the meantime. Mr Smith knew that his client was "a man with a heart of gold — the kind of man who would help anyone who was down and out". What Mr Smith did not know was that his client had had the greatest difficulty in raising the £28-odd: Furnace's bank-manager had recently told him that his overdraft would not be extended; as well as owing money to suppliers, he owed £100 (close to £2,000 in present-day terms) to various acquaintances.

There was a clause in the Brittanic's agreement that made the policy void in the event of Furnace's committing suicide within a year of its inception. That clause became inapplicable at midnight on New Year's Eve.

On the first day of 1933, a Sunday, Furnace threw a party at the house in Crogsland Road. Though he drank nothing stronger than Tizer, he rose late next morning. He strolled to Hawley Crescent, set his employees to work, removed the 1932 calendar from the wall of the dingy office — but did not replace it with a current one — and then popped round to his local café for a chat with friends.

The closest of the friends was Walter Spatchett, a man in his late twenties who, being unwed, lived with his parents in Dartmouth Park Road, to the north of Camden Town, not far from where George Joseph Smith lethally bathed the third of his brides.[1] Spatchett collected rents for Westacott & Sons, a firm of estate managers in Camden Road. He and Furnace had got to know each other when the latter, directly before starting his own business, had worked as a handyman for Westacott's. Furnace owed Spatchett about £60.

The two friends left the café together, Furnace to go home for lunch, Spatchett to continue collecting rents — till shortly

[1] See *The Seaside Murders* (Allison & Busby, 1985).

before half-past three, when he deposited his takings at Lloyds Bank in Camden High Street. During the next couple of hours, as well as collecting a few more rents, he visited builders to receive commission on work that Westacott's had put their way. At five, while sitting in a builder's office, he jotted down and added up — to £35 — his late-afternoon takings. He turned down the offer of a cup of tea, saying that he had one last call to make.

The call was upon Sam Furnace at his shack in Hawley Crescent.

All of his friend's employees had gone home by the time Spatchett arrived.

If anyone heard the explosion of the .45 bullet that tore into his back, killing him probably at once, they may have ascribed it to a faulty engine of a passing motor-vehicle.

Having crammed the corpse within the knee-hole of the desk, Furnace locked up, walked home, ate supper with May and the children, saw the children to bed, staying with them while they said their prayers, listened to a play of *Jane Eyre* on the wireless, and then had an early night.

Up bright and early the next morning, he took May a cup of tea in bed, kissed her fondly, and returned to Hawley Crescent, arriving there before any of his workmen. Among his several chores, perhaps the most taxing (considering that the contorted corpse of Walter Spatchett, by now entirely stiff from *rigor mortis*, was rather a tight fit within the knee-hole of the desk) was the draping over and tucking in around the corpse of an old Melton overcoat that he had thought to bring from home.

During the morning, a workman, entering the office to enquire regarding a task he had been set, was prompted by Furnace's uncomfortable-looking, legs-sideways perching on his desk-stool to ask a second question, viz., "What's that bundle under there?" — to which Furnace replied that he had had some cement delivered and couldn't think where else to stow it.

Meanwhile, the dead man's father had visited the police station in Hornsey Road to report that his son was missing, and had been told to come back in the evening if Walter still hadn't turned up.

It was about seven in the evening when Mr Spatchett Senior, having done a day's work as a chauffeur, returned to the station.

By that time, the yard in Hawley Crescent was deserted save for its tenant, and he was busy with preparations towards his intention of becoming The Late Samuel James Furnace without putting himself to the inconvenience of dying. Not necessarily in this order, he prised the legs of the corpse into a sitting position and sat it on the desk-stool, transferred cash, excluding coppers, from the dead man's pockets to his own, appropriated Walter's gold wrist-watch, splashed the body with oil from the hanging lamp, poured paint on and around the body, made a pyre of wood-shavings and suppliers' invoices around the stool, and wrote a note in pencil: "Goodbye to all. No work, no money. Sam J. Furnace."

After pinning the note to the table in the other room, he ignited the pyre, picked up his bag of tools, and left the shack, locking both doors behind him. He didn't travel far — just a few blocks to a lodging-house in Princess Road, leading towards Regent's Park, where he booked a room under the name of Roy Rogers.

He can hardly have reached the lodging-house when a small child, the daughter of residents of Hawley Crescent, trespassed into the yard, saw flames through a window of the shack, and straightway scampered home to tell her mum. The fire brigade, though soon on the scene, arrived after amateur extinguishers had broken down both doors, dowsed the flames, and observed — only vaguely through the smoke — a body on the stool by the desk. Masked firemen hauled the body out. Much of the clothing had been consumed, and parts of the rest were fused with the skin; the head, being erased of features, was resemblant of an under-inflated rugby ball. Subsequent to the transfer of the remains to St Pancras Mortuary, Furnace's note (which, but for the early alarm given by the little girl, would surely have been destroyed) was found by one of his workmen.

The yard on the morning after
(*By permission of the Commissioner of the Metropolitan Police*)

Though the dead man's face lacked personification,
Furnace's lodger William Abbott was driven to the mortuary
to see if he recognized it — which he did at once, saying that it
was, without doubt, that of Furnace.

May was told that she was a widow.

Next morning, before it was light, her dear departed left the
lodging-house in Princess Road and embarked on a circular
tour, during which he tossed his revolver into the Regent's
Canal, flung its holster into a field at Dagenham, on the
eastern approaches to London, and bought himself a new suit.

Long before when — darkness having fallen again — he
slipped back into the lodging-house, the police had changed
his status from that of suicide victim to that of prime suspect in
a murder case. The change had come about because Bentley
Purchase, the coroner for St Pancras, having questioned the

191

divisional police-surgeon's assumption that the man found *seated* in the shack had died from burning, had himself looked at the body — and noticed a bullet-hole near the top of the lumbar region. Purchase's announcement of his find had caused the local police to look at the few charred and water-logged contents of the dead man's pockets: two items in particular, one being a Post Office savings book (examination of which showed that it was made out in the name of a Mr W. Spatchett) and the other a wallet (examination of which revealed, among other financially-valueless contents, remnants of letters to someone also called Spatchett). Confirmation of the fact that the dead man was Walter Spatchett, reported missing the day before, had come from, *inter alios*, his dentist, who, having been brought to the mortuary, looked for and instantly recognized a peculiar tooth in the upper jaw.

What was to become the most publicised man-hunt since the hue and cry for Doctor Crippen began without benefit of banner-headlines: the information that the police issued to the press eschewed any mention of murder, saying only that Furnace was "wanted to be interviewed" by Scotland Yard regarding the fire in the shack, and giving a description of him, that reading, in part:

> Height, five feet ten and a half inches; fair complexion; fair hair, thin in front; hazel eyes, full face, and a square jaw. . . . When last seen, he was wearing a navy-blue suit, new light-blue shirt and collar to match, lightish-brown overcoat fully belted, grey trilby hat with black band and straight brim, tilted over right eye, light-brown socks and black shoes; the Discharged Serviceman's Badge (the silver badge) on the right lapel of his overcoat.

Despite the discreet wording of the police bulletin, and the absence of any offer of financial reward for help, the search for Furnace at once, and increasingly, tickled the public's imagination. In those days, long before housey-housey was turned into catchpenny Bingo, popular newspapers sought to minimize the sag in summertime sales by offering quids, even fivers, to recognizers of men given names like Lobby Lud whose descriptions and approximate locations had been published in the current issues; and so the self-same papers, viewing Furnace as an out-of-season gift-horse — and ignoring the fact that, so far as the police knew, he was carrying a loaded revolver — cajoled their readers into treating him as if he were a Lobby Lud. Every day while Furnace was at large, at least a hundred claimed sightings of him were reported to Scotland Yard: he was "seen" in just about every part of the land; in Southern Ireland, too; and, as Continental and American papers picked up the story, in those places as well.

On Friday, 6 January — the second full day of the search — the police heard from Mrs Agnes Woolf that a man who had called himself Roy Rogers but whom she now thought was Furnace had stayed at her lodging-house in Princess Road, Camden Town, from Tuesday night until noon on Thursday, when he had left, saying that he had to go to the Essex town of Southend-on-Sea. During the Thursday afternoon, she had received a telegram, marked as having been handed in at the main post office in Southend: "BROTHER ILL RE-LET ROOM RETURNING MONDAY — R. ROGERS."

Detectives who went to Princess Road found that Mrs Woolf's departed lodger had left behind him (*a*) fingerprints that matched those of Furnace, (*b*) a bag of tools (promptly identified as Furnace's by one of his workmen), and (*c*) a navy-blue suit – which, in the light of the combined evidential strength of finds (*a*) and (*b*), indicated that part of the circulated description of Furnace was probably misleading: relying upon Mrs Woolf's recollection of her lodger's going-away costume, the police issued an amended description which, in the "last seen wearing" section, referred not only to a new brown suit but also to "a double-breasted trench-coat with a sliding belt and brown and red check lining with brown leatherette binding".

Those sartorial clues formed an addendum to a message sent post-haste to the Essex Constabulary. Within an hour, road-blocks were set up around Southend, there was a patrol at the railway station, and inquiries were being made at the few hotels and many guest-houses. Presuming that some system was applied to those inquiries, they must have begun on the outskirts and worked inwards, for it was not until the Saturday afternoon that officers arrived at a guest-house in Hartington Road, in the centre of the town, and learned from the landlady, a Mrs Lilley, that a man answering Furnace's description, her guest for two days, had settled his bill and departed at about midday.

Having established that the man was Furnace, the detective of the Metropolitan Police who was leading the hunt assumed — and would brook no querying of the assumption — that his quarry had escaped from Southend. The detective's muddle-headedness and pig-headedness cannot be excused either by the fact that he was a sufferer from an outbreak of influenza that was sweeping the country or by the fact that he, being close to retirement, was giving more thought to the memoirs he had been commissioned to write than to the job he was being paid to do. Telling the Chief Constable of Essex that the assistance of his force was no longer needed, he had himself driven back to London.

There, he sifted through the sifting from the notes of reported sightings, offers of help from clairvoyants and lunatics, and catch-me-if-you-can messages from fun-seeking counterfeit-Furnaces — and then gave orders for lavish expenditure of police manpower on leads that he considered worthy of pursual. One of the orders was so extreme — a "first" in the history of the Metropolitan Police — as to require the approval of the Commissioner, Lord Trenchard: it was for the stopping of every vehicle travelling on main roads from the capital towards the south coast. The order — engendered by an anonymous tip-off that Furnace, back in town after his visit to the Essex seaside, intended to board a vessel bound for France — was carried out on Sunday the 8th. Meanwhile, the Met's few surplus wireless-cars were used in yet another "comb-out" of lodging-houses in and around Camden Town. Perhaps needless to mention, the extreme visibility of the police's desire to find Furnace had by now forced them to say *why* they wanted to find him: bulletins

METROPOLITAN POLICE.

MURDER

WANTED

For the wilful murder of **Walter Spatchett**, whose dead body was found on the 3rd January, 1933, in a shed at the rear of 30, Hawley Crescent, Camden Town, London, occupied as an office by the wanted man.

SAMUEL JAMES FURNACE, born 1890, about 6 feet, well built and set up, complexion fair, hair fair (thin in front), eyes hazel, full face, square jaw, gunshot wounds on left leg and both arms, long scar on right bicep shewing marks of 13 stitches, 1 tooth missing in front upper jaw which may be replaced by false tooth. When last seen on the 7th January, 1933, was wearing a brown suit, black shoes, light trench coat with sliding belt, brown and red check lining edged with brown leatherette binding. He has also a brown overcoat, a grey soft felt hat and a bluish coloured cap. Possesses a fair sum of money. In possession of a revolver. He has passed in the name of Raymond Rogers but might assume any other name.

He might seek employment in the building and decorating trade as a foreman or workman, or in the mercantile marine as a steward or seaman and may take lodgings at a boarding house, apartment house, coffee house, cottage, or any place taking male lodgers.

A warrant for his arrest has been issued and extradition will be applied for.

Any person having knowledge of his whereabouts is requested to inform the nearest Police Station at once.

Metropolitan Police Office
New Scotland Yard S.W.1
9th January, 1933

TRENCHARD,

The Commissioner of Police of the Metropolis

from Scotland Yard proclaimed that he was WANTED FOR MURDER. (Subsequent bulletins were illustrated with three snapshots of Furnace — none of which, it was afterwards admitted, looked much like him, and each of which could have been mistaken for a picture of one member of a trio. The publication of the snaps gave rise to a steep increase in the number of men eyed with suspicion by amateur sleuths, trailed by venturesome urchins, and actually required by policemen to prove that they were not Samuel J. Furnace. A businessman of Northampton, so prominent in that town as to be one of its Rotarians but unfortunate enough to bear a faint resemblance to one of the pictures, was stopped three times by the police during a journey of less than thirty miles to Leicester.)

On the evening of Monday the 9th, for the first time ever, the BBC broadcast an appeal for information regarding the whereabouts of a man "wanted for wilful murder". At about the same time, the detective in charge of the hunt telephoned the Chief Constable of Essex, asking him for further and far more assistance: the visiting by members of his force of every single place of lodging in the county. The detective also asked for a squad of Essex officers, all armed, to join up with a squad of armed Metropolitan policemen at Grays, thence to proceed to the village of Laindon, where, according to apparently reliable information received, Furnace was hiding in a farm-shed. By the time the two squads combined at eleven o'clock, the whole of Essex was swathed by dense fog; and so it took the men two hours to find their way to Laindon, and another hour to locate the shed and, gropingly, surround it. A man *was* dossing there — but he was not Furnace. By one of those coincidences that crop up in almost all extended murder cases, the man, an unemployed labourer who had got on his bike to look for work, hailed from Camden Town and knew Furnace well.

Throughout the rest of the week, the search for Furnace, already red-hot, hotted up still more: ships preparing to leave Cardiff, Liverpool and Southampton were scoured; trains were stopped; cinema programmes were interrupted while the audiences were peered at; spectators at football matches were loud-spokenly asked to stare at their neighbours.

Not without reason, the homes of some relatives and friends of the wanted man were kept under surveillance. And there is little doubt that mail addressed to those relatives and friends was perused by the police prior to its delivery.

On Saturday, 14 January, Charles Tuckfield, a brother-in-law of Furnace's, received a letter at his home in Harringay, north-east of Camden Town. The envelope was postmarked "SOUTHEND, 14 JAN 33". Evidently, the letter had been posted late the night before and (as the Royal Mail was then reasonably efficient) had caught the first post to London. It seems likely that Mr Tuckfield was meant to notice, and did so, that the envelope, with his name and address written on it in pencil, had been unsubtly opened and carelessly resealed. But even supposing that he was unobservant of the tampering, he would no doubt have compared his public duty with the responsibilities of in-lawship, found the latter wanting, and told the police what they were waiting for him to tell them. According to the story that he later sold to the *News of the World*:

> I went cold when I saw the little envelope on the passage floor. I knew from whom and where it came. My fingers trembled so that I could hardly pick it up. Sam had made no attempt to disguise the writing. "Mr Charles Tuckfield" — there it was in a hand too familiar to be mistaken.
>
> "Charlie, who's it from?" my wife called from the kitchen in a whisper that told me that she, too, suspected.
>
> "Can't you guess?" I answered.
>
> "Yes," she said. "It's from — it's from — *him*. Oh, my God!"
>
> For a moment neither of us knew what to do or say. We just stared at the letter. Then — "Open it," said my wife. "We've got nothing to be afraid of."
>
> I slit the envelope carefully, and pulled out two single sheets of tinted paper. The letter was in pencil, and we read it together.

> Dear Charlie, — Just a line to you in hope that I shall be able to see a friend before I end it all.
>
> I am writing to you because I know they will watch May for a long time.

I am at Southend, quite near the station, making out I have been ill with the 'flu, so have been able to stay in all the week.

I am far from well through want of sleep. I don't think I have slept one hour since the accident happened. I will tell you all about it when I see you.

Now, what I want you to do is not for me, but for May and the kiddies. My days are numbered. I want you to come down Sunday, on your own, please. Catch the 10.35 from Harringay Park; that gets you down in Southend at 12.8. Come out of the station, walk straight across the road, and down the opposite road; walk down on the left side.

I will see you. I am not giving my address in case you are followed. Just walk slowly down.

If you come will you bring me 15½ shirt and two collars — any colour will do. Also one pair of socks, dark ones, and one comb. I think that is all now. Don't let anyone know, only Nell [Tuckfield's wife]. If possible say you have to work or something.

Best of luck. Mine is gone. H. FARMER.

Leaving his wife to recover from the shock, Tuckfield walked to the police station in Holmes Road, Kentish Town, and asked to see one of the officers assigned to the Furnace case:

"What's the letter?" the detective asked, pointing to the envelope in my hand.

"That's what I've come about," I told him. "It's from Southend — from Sam Furnace, my brother-in-law."

"Exactly what I thought," he said, but what he thought he didn't explain. . . . He took the letter, read it, and put it in his pocket. He told me to say nothing to anybody, but return to the station at 5.30 that night.

When Tuckfield re-presented himself, he was told:

"You will do exactly as Furnace asks. You will go to Southend by the train he suggests, and take the parcel of clothing with you. Find the road as quickly as you can, and keep your eyes open for his signal. Then you can leave it to us. We will do the rest."

And so, shortly after noon on the following day, Tuckfield walked down Whitegate Road — which was only two blocks from Hartington Road, where Furnace had lodged with Mrs Lilley at the start of his stay in Southend. As Tuckfield came abreast of No. 11, the lace-curtains over the front-room window parted — just sufficiently to reveal a sheet of paper on which was writ large the name SAM. The door opened as he approached it. He went inside. The door closed.

All of a sudden, detectives — both Metropolitan and of the Essex Constabulary — crowded the ends of Whitegate Road. One of their number, rudimentarily musical and very brave, wandered towards No. 11: masquerading as a busker, he played on a fiddle "Roses Are Blooming in Picardy", the only tune he was at all sure of, while slyly examining the premises; when an old lady came out of a nearby house and offered him a penny, he, without interrupting either his fiddling or his examining, advised her to f--k off back inside. Meanwhile, other detectives, all carrying firearms, made their way through the diminutive front gardens on the same side as No. 11 to the houses flanking it, and, once the doors had been opened in response to reticent knocks, enlisted the aid of the residents. They learned that the tenant of No. 11 was a Mrs Charlotte Shaw; that she was a sixty-year-old widow; that she took in paying guests.

Charles Tuckfield emerged at half-past one. By then, the officers in No. 9 had prevailed upon the lady of the house to pop next door and bring Mrs Shaw back with her, under the pretext that her advice was needed concerning a recipe for seed-cake. No sooner was Mrs Shaw in No. 9, staring bewilderedly at the full house of bowler-hatted men holding revolvers and rifles, than she was told to forget about seed-cake: she was to go home and, as casually as she could manage, make certain that the kitchen-door was unlocked — then, when she got a signal to do so, perform a further small errand.

Mrs Shaw did as she had been told. As soon as half a dozen detectives were in the kitchen, a nod from one of them prompted her to walk along the passage, tap on the door of the

THE DAILY MIRROR, Monday, January 16, 1933.

Daily Mirror

THE DAILY PICTURE NEWSPAPER WITH THE LARGEST NET SALE

NEW TEST SENSATION —Page 3

WIRELESS PAGE 20 AMUSEMENTS PAGE 20

No. 9,004   Registered at the G.P.O. as a Newspaper   MONDAY, JANUARY 16, 1933   One Penny

FIRESIDE ARREST OF FURNACE

Exclusive "Daily Mirror" Story of His Life in Hiding at a Southend Boarding House

CHARGED WITH MURDER AFTER SEARCH THAT LASTED ELEVEN DAYS

After one of the sternest and most far-flung man-hunts on record, Samuel James Furnace, the Chalk Farm builder, was arrested yesterday while seated by the fireside in a Southend boarding house.

He had been in the house for nine out of the eleven days on which the police were searching for him. His landlady, Mrs. Charlotte Susan Shaw, a widow of sixty, thought he was recovering from the 'flu.

Furnace, who was brought handcuffed to London last night, was charged with the murder on January 3 of Walter Spatchett, the young rent collector, whose charred body was found in a shed used by Furnace as an office at the back of a house in Hawley-crescent, Chalk Farm, N.W. Furnace will appear at Marylebone Police Court this morning.

"MR. FARMER OF LONDON"

Landlady Tells How She Nursed a Supposed Invalid

(EXCLUSIVE)

When a *Daily Mirror* reporter talked to Mrs. Shaw last night he found her still bewildered by the swift turn of the day's events.

"The whole thing has been a terrible shock to me," she said. "Furnace had been so exceptionally pleasant all the time he had been at my house. I thought he was an invalid and I had treated him as one, and did my best to look after him.

"He came to my house a week last Saturday. He seemed a quiet, presentable sort of man, and when he asked me for a room I had no hesitation in letting one to him.

"He told me then that he was convalescent. 'I am just getting over a severe attack of influenza,' Mrs. Shaw, he said, 'and the doctor has sent me down here to recuperate.'

Wrapped in Blankets

At the time he was looking pale, though not noticeably so, but as the days went on he seemed to get worse.

"All the time he was with me he only left his room twice. On several occasions I lost him limping back and tried to persuade him to eat, and more than once I wrapped him round with blankets and urged him to keep himself warm.

(Continued on page 2)

Mrs. Shaw, landlady of the boarding house in which Furnace was found. She states that she looked after him "like a mother."

The boarding-house where Furnace was living for the past week. He stayed indoors, saying he was unwell.

Samuel Furnace.

An aerial view of Southend-on-Sea, showing: (A) the White gate-road where Furnace was found and arrested (B) the L.M.S. railway station, (D) Alexandra-street, in which the police station is situated, (E) the beginning of High-street and (F) the pier.

Walter Spatchett, victim of the Chalk Farm blazing-shed tragedy. Furnace has been charged with his murder.

front room and straightway push it wide, saying, "Did you call?" Her instructor had neglected to tell her to step aside, and so she got a nasty bruise on the elbow as the detectives galloped past her, their guns levelled at Samuel Furnace, who was sitting in an armchair by the fire, reading about himself in the *Sunday People*.

Once he had regained his composure — by which time he was handcuffed and had been searched — he seemed relieved that he had at last been caught. Corroborated by Mrs Shaw, he said that he had been in the house since the Saturday before last, directly after his short stay at Mrs Lilley's.

The handcuffs were briefly released so that he could put on his coat, and then he was taken to Southend Police Station; two officers stayed behind to search his room. During the drive to London, he admitted that he had killed Walter Spatchett but insisted that the revolver had gone off by accident. As the car was travelling along Camden Road, he pointed out the place from which he had thrown the revolver into the Regent's Canal. (The weapon was retrieved next day.) At Kentish Town Police Station, after being charged and cautioned, he made a statement. His version of his final meeting with Walter Spatchett was as follows:

> We stood talking for five minutes, after which I told him I had a revolver. He appeared interested, so I showed it to him. He took the revolver and cocked it. I noticed what he had done and told him it was loaded. . . . He handed it back to me, saying, "You had better see to it as you know more about them than me, and I have to get back to the office." I was showing him out through the office door with the gun in my left hand, and as he was going through the door the gun went off and shot him. He fell to the ground groaning. I realised my position and lost my head. . . .

Furnace, still wearing his coat, was locked in cell No. 3.

At seven o'clock next morning, Police Constable George Partridge peeped through the spy-hole in the door of the cell. He saw Furnace pull something from the lining of his coat: a small medicine-bottle. By the time Partridge entered the cell, Furnace had swallowed the spirits of salts from the bottle, was already writhing in agony on the stone floor. He was taken to

St Pancras Hospital, but all that a doctor could do was to ease his pain with morphia. He told the doctor that he had bought the spirits of salts on Twelfth Night, soon after his arrival in Southend. The only other words he was heard to utter before his death in the early hours of the following morning, Tuesday, 17 January, were: "My wife. . . ."

Two inquests followed. That on Furnace was largely taken up by questions, awkward and embarrassing for the police witnesses, regarding his possession of the spirits of salts. That on Spatchett resulted in the verdict that he had been murdered by Furnace.

It seems likely that Furnace's crime was doubly emulative. He would not have been the first murderer — nor the last — to have been inspired to try to use successfully methods employed unsuccessfully by much-publicized predecessors. His crime is reminiscent both of that of Alfred Arthur Rouse (who in 1931 was hanged after it was proved that he had killed and roasted an unknown hitch-hiker in the hope that the sparse remains would be misidentified as his, Rouse's, thus enabling him to start a new life) and of that of Sidney Fox (who in 1930 was hanged after it was proved that he had strangled his mother, then ignited her surroundings, all within the space of half an hour before insurance on her life ran out).[1]

Though Furnace's life-policy was deemed null and void, on the ground that "no person can benefit himself or his estate by a felonious act", the Britannic Assurance Co., keen to be reported as being a sympathetic organization, announced that it would make an *ex-gratia* payment to his widow, May.

Apart from the mourners, a good time was had by all of the hundreds of people who attended Furnace's funeral in East Finchley. A busker (of course not the temporary one who had interfered with the lunch-time serenity of Whitegate Road, Southend, a few days before) played jazz music in competition with the organist's rendering of "Mine Eyes Have Seen the Glory". Furnace had never expressed a preference for a means of his disposal, and so it was at May's request that his body was buried, not cremated.

[1] See *The Seaside Murders* (Allison & Busby, 1985).

The Thirty-Guinea Murder

Jonathan Goodman

TILL A MONTH OR SO AGO, I had never even ruffled the pages of a book on the history of trades unionism. Then, for a reason that will soon be clear to you, I remedied the omission, skipping through early chapters of half a dozen such books before consulting the indexes.

Hundreds of place-names that, depending on one's "leftishness" or "rightishness", made up a roll of honour or dishonour. But no sign of either of the names I had expected — or rather, hoped — to find: Apethorn and Woodley.

In 1831, those villages, lying between Stockport and Hyde in the county of Cheshire, were the sites of cotton-mills owned by one Samuel Ashton. He lived in a mansion, Pole Bank Hall, which stood (and still stands) on the hill of Werneth Low, a mite over a mile from Woodley and slightly farther from the smaller and more northerly Apethorn. By the standards of the time, Samuel Ashton was a humanitarian cotton lord — not unlike his friend, "Ready-money Jack" Leech, who was the talk of the area for his project of building houses for the workers at his mill in Stalybridge.

But despite Samuel Ashton's "paternalism", there had been unrest at both of his mills — prompting authoritarian mill-owners to comment that "the more you gave workers, the more they wanted". There had been intermittent lay-offs and periods of short-time working at the mills, and in December 1830 a number of employees at Apethorn — among them, a young man called William Mosley — had been sacked.

Resentment at cuts in wages ... fear of unemployment: reasons for some of the unrest, no doubt. Some but not all of it. Slight discontent may have been fanned into downright hostility by outside agitators, or "firebrands", whose soapbox oratory had as its nub the contrast between the earnings of the mill-hands and the profits of the cotton lords.

And Samuel Ashton may unwittingly have contributed to his troubles by deciding to take life easier, passing day-to-day control of the Woodley mill to his twenty-four-year-old son Thomas, and giving his younger son James "learning-by-doing" management training at Apethorn. Perhaps the two new brooms swept too clean for the liking of some of the workers.

A need for overtime at the Apethorn mill on the night of Monday, 3 January 1831, created a social worry for James Ashton, who had arranged to escort a girl-friend to a soirée in Stockport. He talked things over with his brother, who eventually agreed to look in at the mill to ensure that there was no slacking.

And so, at seven o'clock, Thomas Ashton set off from Pole Bank Hall. He was on foot, because the family's coach was being used by his father.

He did not get far.

Only minutes after his departure, his dead body was found in a ditch near the entrance to the grounds of the Hall. He had been shot in the chest with a double-charged gun of some kind. It appeared that death had been instantaneous, for his right hand was clenched in the pocket of his greatcoat, the fabric of which was scorched, showing that the shooting had been at point-blank range.

There was a hue and cry for the murderers.

Murderers? Yes, so it seemed. Several witnesses attested to the fact that three men, walking together, had climbed

Werneth Low just before the crime. And a labourer on a farm near Pole Bank Hall had seen three men rushing through the fields shortly afterwards.

Even before the inquest was opened at the Boy & Barrel Inn at Gee Cross, Hyde, a reward of £500 was offered for information leading to the arrest and conviction of the culprits. Then a Royal Proclamation was issued, offering a further £1,000. £1,500 — a fortune in those days. Clearly, not only the cotton lords of Cheshire and Lancashire but also many members of parliament saw worrying implications — frightening ones, even — from the murder of Thomas Ashton. Since few people could have known that Thomas would be abroad that night, there was strong reason for concluding that the murderers had lain in wait for *any* member of the Ashton family to appear on the lonely road.

The offer of the rewards brought no worthwhile information. One can surmise that this increased the trepidation of the privileged minority who could afford to be worried. Did the sparsity of information indicate a conspiracy of silence? Were people who knew the identity of the murderers so in favour of the crime that they were prepared to turn down the chance of living on Easy Street?

Over three years went by. Then, in April 1834, a convict in Derby Gaol, seeking to minimize his stay there, volunteered to be a "grass". Referring to the murder on Werneth Low, he suggested that the authorities would be "well advised" to speak to twenty-six-year-old William Mosley and his brother Joseph, aged thirty-one, who was "as daft as a brush".

William Mosley was soon persuaded to save his own neck by turning King's Evidence against his brother and twenty-two-year-old James Garside. According to his version of the events, on New Year's Eve, 1830, he and Joseph, both of whom were planning to trudge to Macclesfield in search of work, were having a drink in the Stag's Head at Marple, close to their home. James Garside joined them. He said, without giving details, that he knew of a way of making a lot of money. The brothers were to meet him at Marple Bridge in the early afternoon of the next day; from there, they would walk to Compstall Brow, midway between Marple and Werneth Low, for a rendezvous with two men.

As they had nothing better to do, the Mosleys accompanied Garside to Compstall Brow on New Year's Day. Two strangers appeared. They were well dressed, but William gathered from their speech that they were of the artisan class. He heard little of their conversation with Garside. He was sure, though, that the word *union* was uttered. The sound of someone approaching from the direction of Romiley, to the west, put an abrupt end to the encounter. One of the strangers handed Garside a package, and then, with his companion, ran off down the side of the Brow farther from Romiley.

On the way back to Marple, Garside told the Mosleys that they would each receive ten guineas if they helped him to murder a member of the Ashton family. The blood-money would be paid the day after the job was done. Garside opened the package, revealing a horse-pistol.

Neither of the brothers asked a single question. Perhaps they feared that inquisitiveness would prejudice the unexpected opportunity of having more money in their pockets than they had ever had at one time before.

On the night of 3 January, they stepped from the shadows as soon as Thomas Ashton had passed, thus making sure that he could not run back to Pole Bank Hall — away from James Garside, the man with the gun.

Next day, the three murderers received their wages from the strangers. But before the thirty pieces of gold were distributed, a strange ceremony was enacted. One of the strangers — his name was Stanfield or Schofield, William Mosley believed — produced a receipt book for the men to sign. Then "we all went down on our knees, declaring to God that we would never tell, and praying to God to strike us dead if we did. We did this, one after another, and we all held a knife over each other while we did so."

William Mosley's testimony, foremost among that of some twenty witnesses at the trial at Chester Castle in August 1834, left the jury in no doubt that Joseph Mosley and James Garside were guilty. Garside's defence, if one can call it that, was that William, who had talked himself away from the gallows, had fired the horse-pistol; Joseph put up no defence at all.

Instead of being hanged somewhere close to home, the two men were taken all the way to London, where they were executed outside Horsemonger Lane Gaol. Was their last journey really necessary? What was the purpose of it? An elongation of publicity? A way of disencouraging others who might feel inclined to use extreme means of fighting the bosses?

I am not going to try to answer those questions — nor the one about whether the mysterious strangers were representatives of a fledgling union or men paid by cotton lords perturbed at industrial unrest, willing to sacrifice one of their own to the cause of bringing unionism into disrepute. It is up to a trades-union historian to search for the answers. I just hope that if he comes up with information that doesn't tend to "Tolpuddle-ize" the men punished for the murder of Thomas Ashton, he will not report the findings only to his executive council.

Acknowledgements and Sources

In addition to those given in the text: "The Christmas Sack Murder" is published by permission of the author; "The Ratcliffe Highway Horrors" is from Volume V, Numbers 60 and 61, of *Famous Crimes*, a part-work published circa 1900 by Harold Furniss, Gough Square, London; "Packaged Death", a revised version of an essay that first appeared in the *American Bar Association Journal*, is published by permission of the author; "The Case of Oscar Slater" was published in 1912 by Hodder & Stoughton, London, and the George H. Doran Company, New York; "The Distribution of Hannah Brown" is from a Newgate Calendar; "A Bedroom in Pimlico", an extract from *Victorian Studies in Scarlet* (London, 1970), is published by permission of the author and J.M. Dent & Sons Ltd; "The Slaying of Léon Beron" is from *Murders and Murder Trials, 1812–1912*, published in 1932 by Constable, London; "Murder of a Minder" is from a Newgate Calender; "Sam's New-Year Resolution", which first appeared in the *Police Review*, is published by permission of the author; "The Thirty-Guinea Murder", which first appeared in the *Manchester Evening News*, is published by permission of the author.